Children's Online Behaviour and Safety

Andy Phippen

Children's Online Behaviour and Safety

Policy and Rights Challenges

Andy Phippen
Plymouth Business School
School of Management
Plymouth, United Kingdom

ISBN 978-1-137-57094-9   ISBN 978-1-137-57095-6 (eBook)
DOI 10.1057/978-1-137-57095-6

Library of Congress Control Number: 2016950850

Cover illustration: Pattern adapted from an Indian cotton print produced in the 19th century

Printed on acid-free paper

This Palgrave Macmillan imprint is published by Springer Nature
The registered company is Macmillan Publishers Ltd.
The registered company address is: The Campus, 4 Crinan Street, London, N1 9XW, United Kingdom

FOREWORD

I am delighted to have the opportunity to provide a foreword for this new book that looks at the often complex relationship between enabling children to benefit from technology and the Internet whilst at the same time keeping them safe. In more recent times, with growing interest from policy makers, legislators and politicians, alongside a greater sense of collaboration from industry, we have made great strides forward with regard to safety. However, we are, perhaps, still failing to appreciate that young people should be a primary stakeholder in this space, not just a passive observer to have our decisions placed upon them.

Within the online safety community we have worked for many years on this complex balancing act, and, as technologies and behaviours evolve, and more stakeholders take an interest, the balance becomes more difficult to achieve. Of course, we could ensure children and young people are entirely safe from the threats posed by the online world by simply preventing them from going online. However, this is, of course, a ridiculous solution as our focus on safety would completely detract from all of the positives that digital technology and online worlds bring to young people's lives.

Having worked with Andy for many years, and over that time having many discussions with him on this balance, I am so pleased to see that much of this current thinking appears in this book. Over the years we have worked together on many pieces of research, initially, way back in 2006, exploring our respective understandings of how children engage with digital technology and the development of their own coping strategies, before moving on to issues such as the early research work into sexting, understanding issues of the online abuse of teachers, looking at peer learning around online safety, and the, now, annual review of online safety policy and practice in schools across the country, drawing upon the significant and unique 360 degree safe dataset.

Andy's position within the community is somewhat unusual—on the one hand an academic bringing all of the objectivity and understanding of research methodology to his work that academia affords, but on the other hand being incredibly hands on with his work, conducting assemblies, classes, discussion groups, staff development activities and parents forums, to name a few, in order to engage with the community and to pass on his knowledge.

He has always spoken to the whole range of stakeholders, but most importantly he speaks to children, a lot. And not just to deliver "information" sessions, but sitting with them, working with them, answering their questions and, most importantly, listening to them about their practices, beliefs and concerns. It is clear that many children are not afforded this opportunity and relish it. Putting children and their views central to any research is something he has done from the very early days of our working partnership. I must admit, sometimes I am alarmed at the sort of things he hears about, and the sort of questions he is asked (some of which he refers to in this book), but what this grass roots activity does very clearly highlight is that, given the right environment and response, young people will talk about their online lives, and that they have many questions to ask. While we have seen great steps forward in the curriculum and regulatory framework to ensure online safety is addressed, primarily in schools, it still seems rare that young people are afforded these opportunities.

The UK Safer Internet Centre and its constituent partners have seen the development of online safety policy thinking over a number of years now, from the inception of the Byron Review onward. Over this time there has been unprecedented growth in the interest of policy makers and the regulators in online safety issues. While 10 years ago we were calling for inspectorates to consider online safety as a key safeguarding and educational measure in schools, this is now largely in place. David Cameron was the first UK prime minister to deliver a public speech on online safety, and we see a continued commitment from the UK government to address online safety concerns.

Within this book Andy is quite critical of the direction of some policy, albeit acknowledging the increased activity and the positive impacts that come from parallel areas, for example the changes in the OFSTED framework. However, this criticism is constructive and sympathetic to the fact that the changes needed to develop an education system that develops aware, resilient and responsible young people are long term and sometimes at odds with the shorter cycles of policy making and impact measurement. And while I might suggest, and have certainly said to him, that some of his criticism is harsh, I agree that it is crucial that we widen the policy focus around online safety, away from just from the need to protect children from passively accessing certain types of content toward looking at ways to educate and build resilience in all our young people. As technology continues to innovate and become more sophisticated, our online safety education, curriculum and support needs to evolve at the same pace. We need to learn from the limited impact of past preventative approaches in child protection, and ensure that children can recognise risk and apply online safety skills and competencies that we should aim to provide.

As Andy suggests, we need to develop policy that is informed by the evidence base. We are lucky within the UK to have many outstanding academics and practitioners in this field who contribute to a rich understanding of young people's online behaviours and, such is the nature of research, while some of it conflicts, that is not to say it is impossible to use it to inform policy. While it might be understandable that policy makers may respond to gut feelings and media opinion on these issues, as discussed by Andy in this book sometimes we need to step back and acknowledge that just because we believe something to be a fact, this is not necessarily the case. And we also need to recognise that there are many things we still do not understand in depth (e.g. the impact of pornography on the first generation of young people to have such unrestricted access to it). It is therefore important that within the community we continue to encourage research in all its facets and work together to understand how we many best serve children's needs and rights in this area.

But most importantly, we need to use this understanding to develop education, in terms of curricula, resources and support, that is up to date, knowing and relevant for the young people for whom it is intended. We need to support parents who often struggle in this regard as well as our amazing teaching professionals in helping young people understand both the benefits and risks of online technologies, and provide them with opportunities in which they can ask questions without fear of repercussion, to challenge opinions and contribute to the debate, using their own experiences to articulate their thoughts and to know that we understand it is their lives and development we are endeavouring to support, rather than just telling them not to do things or they'll get into trouble.

A central theme within this book is that we cannot use safeguarding arguments to erode children's rights. Children have as much a right to education, to privacy, to a life free from harassment, to be able to access useful and complete information, as anyone else. We cannot argue that, for their own good, some of those rights have to be eroded. Every "online safety" development, whether this be policy, technology or education resource, needs to reflect upon how they will impact on children.

This book is a significant contribution to the online safety community. It is of value not just for the academic community, but also for practitioners and policy makers working in this area. Written in an accessible manner while still being underpinned by hard evidence and academic rigour, it raises some difficult challenges and is sometimes controversial in its thinking. However, at its heart is something all of us in the community should agree with. Children and young people should be at the core of anything related to keeping them safely online.

Director of the UK Safer Internet Centre   David Wright
April 2016

CONTENTS

List of Figures

LIST OF TABLES

CHAPTER 1

What Do We Mean by "Child Online Safety"?

Abstract There is growing concern, given the growth of the Internet and subsequent online technologies, to ensure that, while children and young people are empowered to engage with the digital world, they can do so in a safe and risk free way. The author presents a juxtaposition of the views of adult and child stakeholders in the field of online safety by exploring thinking about what we actually mean by "online safety" and how we might go about achieving this. In reviewing the growing concerns around implementing whatever is meant by "child online safety," the author uses recent UK policy developments (2010–2015) around the theme to illustrate adult stakeholder perspectives, and recommends the need to draw policy from a stronger evidence base with a more powerful youth voice, while stressing the need to ensure children's rights in any attempt to keep them safe online.

Keywords Child online safety · Policy · Children's rights

> *I want to talk about the Internet, the impact it's having on the innocence of our children, how online pornography is corroding childhood and how, in the darkest corners of the Internet, there are things going on that are a direct danger to our children and that must be stamped out.*

> (David Cameron, UK Prime Minister, July 2013; Cameron 2013)

© The Author(s) 2017
A. Phippen, *Children's Online Behaviour and Safety,*
DOI 10.1057/978-1-137-57095-6_1

1

I think there are a lot of things adults stereotype young people for. We don't all do the things you talk about. I know that some of us do, but I think adults exaggerate a lot.

(15-year-old girl, 2015; source: conversation with her about online safety education)

The digital world presents many opportunities and benefits for our young people. In a single generation we have moved from virtually no online technology to an era where digital devices provide them with the opportunities to:

- Find information on anything they like;
- Interact and play games with people on the other side of the world;
- Create content and upload it for anyone to see;
- Connect with friends, family and virtual "friends" (the distinction and quotes are deliberate) through social media via PCs, laptops and mobile devices.

These interactions happen many, many times a day and I am sure we are all familiar with the sight of young people, and indeed those who are older, walking around their neighbourhoods looking not at the world around them but at the digital device they have in their hand. Clearly there are many benefits to this digital world——countless children tell me homework starts and finishes online these days, and keeping in touch with friends and family is easier than ever and, certainly in my experience, young people's enthusiasm for technology can be transformed into lucrative careers.

However, for all of the benefits there are clearly risks associated with online technologies, and these will be explored in depth throughout this book. When considering child protection and online technology, the focus can often lead to a perception of "young persons as victims" with a need to protect them from the external perils that exist—that young people are passive consumers of digital technology, and that a content focus on harm allows us to understand what "safety" is for them. As a by-product of a content focus, we can begin to ensure child safety online before centring on prevention and access control around "harmful" content. In this book I will challenge those perspectives and present a number of different viewpoints that show that young peoples' relationships with technology are far more complex than that of passive consumption. I will explore the potential for solutions where we have less of a clear-cut child protection perspective and where young people are as likely to play the part of abuser or offender in online relationships, even if they aren't aware that they are doing anything offensive or, indeed, illegal, and therefore cannot so readily claim responsible action.

One thing I should state from the start is that I observe two very different perceptions of young people from my work. In general, the adult perspective, whether teacher, parent, member of the children's workforce, journalist or politician, will be one where young people are viewed as a single entity from afar: "Young people need protection from this sort of thing" or "Young people are always doing this." The second perspective comes from young people themselves——in their minds "it is complicated," and they wish to have fora to discuss their online lives and the behaviours and moralities around it. They have questions on legalities, protection, consent and emotional issues such as empathy and respect. Yet, sadly, it seems they rarely get the opportunity to ask these questions.

These two differing perspectives are clearly illustrated in the opening quotes to this chapter. The first, from the UK Prime Minister David Cameron, in a speech that focussed on "The Internet and Pornography" takes the consumption perspective. It uses very direct language to make it clear that we will ensure young peoples' safety online by stamping out the impact a specific type of content—pornography—is having on their lives. It seems to express some definite interpretations of the impact of such content on young people and makes it clear they are being damaged by pornography, and there are parts of the Internet that are a danger to them. He proposes a solution that will prevent this access and therefore remove the problem and danger.

It seems that, in some of the debates we have around these issues, "young people" is used as a term to describe the whole of the population under the age of 18, as if they, as a collective, act in the same way and believe the same things. Yet when I speak to young people themselves, I meet so many different personalities, perspectives, belief systems and behaviours it would be impossible ever to say "Young people think the following..." Yet these are the perspectives we try to impose. While it would seem ridiculous to say, for example, that "25–30 year olds are all sexting," these are the sort of statements made about teenagers (e.g. *Daily Mail* 2012a).

This, of course, makes any approaches to protecting young people from harm online and managing digital risk much more difficult, because one approach might work for some, but not others. However, one consistent experience from my many conversations with young people is that they want to talk about online issues and that they have lots of questions to ask.

Evidence of this comes from the second quote at the start of this chapter, which is drawn from a conversation I had with a 15-year-old girl in a workshop I was running in a school in the South West of England. In recent times schools have been told, and encouraged through regulation, that they need to place online safety in the curriculum and that children need to be educated about such things. This is something we will return to later in this text. As a result, I often get asked by schools to work with their pupils.

In this case, however, I was working with a number of young people from a school where we were discussing how online safety is delivered in their school and how effective they felt it was. In particular, we wanted to explore whether they felt "safety" was an appropriate term and whether they felt that the sort of education they received would achieve safety for them and their peers. I had a long conversation with the girl above, who seemed quite angry about the sort of education she had received—which was very "one way" in nature—and who made some clear statements about the sorts of things young people got up to online. In her words, they had been given "the sexting assembly," "the bullying assembly" and the "stranger danger assembly." However, she seemed most frustrated that "you"—the adults in her life—have preconceived ideas about what young people do online and, in reality, the truth is actually far more complex. While she had peers that might engage in practices such as sexting (see Chap. 5), far more did not, and she was annoyed and frustrated that they were essentially being told "you do this and you should not."

In this five-minute conversation it became very clear that binary, absolute "solutions" to online safety are proposing a one-size-fits-all approach to something that is perhaps not sufficiently understood yet to ensure it to be effective. To take David Cameron's quote, and we will return to that speech in far more detail in Chap. 2, the idea that one can "stamp out" a risk which is poorly understood, with inconclusive evidence underpinning the ideology around prevention, one can see why political rhetoric (i.e. "Something must be done!") can be challenged. Forming definitive policy on the back of weak evidence is always going to be challenging, and rarely effective. The challenge we face in this field is that if we don't understand the behaviours, or the impact of them, how can we attempt to implement solutions that are going to be effective?

So let's start with a simple attempt to define what we mean by online safety for children as it seems to mean different things to politicians than it does to young people themselves. If we consider initially the *Oxford English Dictionary* (OED Online 2016) definition of safety, we have the following: "The condition of being protected from or unlikely to cause danger, risk, or injury."

Therefore, if we take a safety focus within the online environment, we are trying to look at the prevention of harm as a result of issues that occur in the digital world. So for the opening discussions in this book, we will start with the following simple definition for child online safety: "The approaches to ensuring children and young people can engage with online technologies safely" or: "Using digital technology while being protected from danger, risk or injury."

However, while a starting definition is useful, it will become apparent throughout this book that the use of this term does sometimes struggle to address the sorts of matters that arise through young people engaging with digital technology.

A road safety analogy is often used when discussing these concepts, i.e. we teach children about how to cross the road and interact with the highways of our towns and cities in a safe manner. The analogy seems to be that if we can implement safety in this environment into our children's lives, why can't we do the same for the online world?

The key difference between "road safety" and "online safety" is that the road environment is a static one. Within road safety we have a predictable environment (roads, traffic, pedestrians, etc.) and generally repeating behaviours governed by clear rules (e.g. cars drive on the roads, their direction is determined by the side of the road on which they travel, they stop at designated signals). It is unlikely that, as the years go by, the road safety environment will evolve a great deal—we certainly don't see radical change with the roads and highways.

When we go online, the environment is constantly evolving and changing—as connectivity speeds increase, the potential for new devices and technologies evolves and the social adoption of those technologies results in unpredictable take up and behaviours. If we look back only 10 years, the idea of a 20 Mbps plus connection in the home would have been seen as extraordinary, as would a device capable of streaming video across a mobile network. We have an environment where developers produce new applications and functionality without much thought for how it might be used and abused once released. While it would be unthinkable for a car manufacturer to release a vehicle without safety features, and without well-documented risk analysis, such expectations are not placed on the software industry.

This is not to say that it is solely a developer's responsibility to consider every possible social use of an application it has developed, as this can be extremely difficult to do. For example, when the first text message was sent in 1992, no one predicted this would become one of the most popular forms of personal communication worldwide 20 years later. However, the point is that, while the road safety analogy is often used, it is far more complex to apply it in a fluid, constantly evolving environment.

With online safety, do we sufficiently understand the risks and dangers that can *guarantee* that if young people are to follow a number of rules and practices they will be free from danger and risk online? How can policy makers, educators and other stakeholders (more on that later) put the necessary safeguards in place, whether they be technological, legislative, educational or social, to *ensure* online safety, without a clear understanding of the issues young people face?

In this book we will be exploring the nature of child online safety in the UK, from the perspectives of both policy and practice, over the last five years. The UK focus is simply because, as a result of this text drawing significantly from my own evidence base, and my work taking place mainly in the UK, it is natural that the policy perspective should also come from this location. However, that is not to say that the evidence presentation, and the arguments made, are only relevant to the UK—there is nothing particularly different or special about the UK population and policy makers that imply this work is only of interest to those within the UK. Given the activity around child online safety over the last five years, and given the evidence base presented, the UK environment allows us to achieve a broader context—to explore how a Government responds to changes in society beyond their control.

This is an interesting period of time in which to explore these issues because the last five years have, arguably, been the most active in the policy area around child online safety and education in the Westminster government's history. Following the Byron Review toward the end of the last Labour government (Byron 2008), coupled with the increased diversity of Internet enabled devices and services, as well as media interest in the potential risks and harm associated with young people's online experiences, the present government has been far more engaged in debate, discussion and legislative response around the topic than ever before.

While we will explore policy evolution in more depth in Chap. 2 and also throughout this book, it is worth considering what we might view as the starting point for this debate early within our discussion, as this will lay the foundations. The Bryon Review, or "Safer Children in a Digital World," was commissioned in 2007 by the then UK Prime Minister Gordon Brown to look at the issues around young people going online and the associated potential benefits and risks. Arguably this was the first time the UK government had invested in a detailed and focussed review on children and digital technology, and the impacts. Conducted by leading child psychologist Professor Tanya Byron, the review sought to look at the evidence around risks to children as a result of exposure to online content and video games. The full report, published in March 2008, presented the following conclusions:

- *The Internet and video games are very popular with children and young people and offer a range of opportunities for fun, learning and development.*
- *But there are concerns over potentially inappropriate material, which range from content (e.g. violence) through to contact issues and the conduct of children in the digital world.*
- *Debates and research in this area can be highly polarised and charged with emotion.*
- *Having considered the evidence I believe we need to move from a discussion about the media "causing" harm to one which focuses on children and young people, what they bring to technology and how we can use our understanding of how they develop to empower them to manage risks and make the digital world safer.*
- *There is a generational digital divide which means that parents do not necessarily feel equipped to help their children in this space—which can lead to fear and a sense of helplessness. This can be compounded by a risk-averse culture where we are inclined to keep our children "indoors" despite their developmental needs to socialise and take risks.*
- *While children are confident with the technology, they are still developing critical evaluation skills and need our help to make wise decisions.*
- *In relation to the Internet we need a shared culture of responsibility with families, industry, government and others in the public and third sectors all playing their part to reduce the availability of potentially*

harmful material, to restrict access to it by children and to increase children's resilience.

- *I propose that we seek to achieve gains in these three areas by having a national strategy for child Internet safety which involves better self-regulation and better provision of information and education for children and families.*
- *In relation to video games, we need to improve on the systems already in place to help parents restrict children's access to games which are not suitable for their age.*
- *I propose that we seek to do that by reforming the classification system and pooling the efforts of the games industry, retailers, advertisers, console manufacturers and online gaming providers to raise awareness of what is in games and enable better enforcement.*
- *Children and young people need to be empowered to keep themselves safe —this isn't just about a top-down approach. Children will be children, pushing boundaries and taking risks. At a public swimming pool we have gates, put up signs, lifeguards and shallow ends, but we also teach children how to swim.*

While the focus of the review was very much on the impact of content upon the child, it very clearly made the case for a multi-stakeholder perspective on addressing online safety and proposed a proactive approach where children were key stakeholders. In addition, it very clearly stated that little national coordination around this area existed, but which was needed. It is also interesting to note the view of young people as active participants in the online space, rather than passive consumers, and the proposed refocus away from prevention toward understanding child development and how that might facilitate safety.

Since the Byron Review was conducted there has been far more significant take up of digital technology by children and young people, as a result of greater connectivity and the availability of more accessible devices such as smartphones and tablets. For example, the OFCOM Media Literacy report in 2014 (OFCOM 2014) stated that around 10 % of three to four year old children owned their own tablet computer, a device which was very much in its infancy when the review was released (iPads not being released by Apple until 2010) which, again, demonstrates the constantly changing environment in which online safety sits.

Moving to our own study period, between 2010 and 2015, there have been a number of significant policy developments:

- The All Party Inquiry into Child Online Safety, which ran from 2011 to 2012, chaired by Claire Perry MP.
- David Cameron's speech on child online safety, in July 2013, and a follow up speech at WeProtect in 2014.
- Changes to the UK school's regulator (OFSTED) inspection process, particularly around safeguarding, which was put in place in September 2012 with a subsequent new framework for inspection in 2015.
- Parliamentary discussions around sex and relationship education and personal, social and health education, including the rejection of compulsory sex and relationship education in 2013 by the House of Lords, and the Education Select Committee's call for it in 2015.

All of these will be explored in far more detail in Chap. 2 but are introduced here to show that there has been significant policy-level activity in this area. However, a central argument in this book is that, while there has clearly been policy activity, what has changed to improve the likelihood of achieving our definition of online safety?

In exploring these issues and the differences between policy and practice I will draw predominantly from my own experience of working with young people about how technology affects their lives and also wider discussion and observation around this field of "online child safety." As mentioned above, I spend a lot of my working life talking to young people about their use of technology, all the way from speaking to reception aged children (four to five years old) about what technologies they have and how they use them, to far more complex and detailed conversations with teenagers about their online lives and the rich interaction they have in their social worlds as facilitated by digital technology. My first experiences in talking with children about these issues date back to 2006 (Lacohee et al. 2006) where, as part of a project exploring the motivations for the public engagement of technology, we made a decision to speak to young people from a number of different schools about their own relationships with emerging online services. The impression we received was one of technologically engaged young people lacking in awareness of the risks involved, receiving little education around the area, and whose coping and resilience approaches were generally peer led and somewhat ineffective.

This has led to a long period of study around children and technology. Generally speaking I do not conduct "planned" research projects where as a researcher I establish a context to address a particular question. More it is *an ethnography of children and digital technology*, allowing for discussions to flow and evolve as a result of the activities I am carrying out. With its foundation in ethnographic approaches such as Peter Woods's seminal book (Woods 1979), the work draws upon different perspectives from the stakeholders around child online safety. While the focus is on young people themselves, the approach allows an exploration of the tensions between policy and education with parents, teachers, senior managers and others in the children's workforce.

Generally, these conversations emerge from other activities either in school or other youth settings. For example, in the last year I have carried out assemblies, classes and workshops with over 2000 young people across the country. The sorts of activities I have been involved with range from workshops as part of a "collapsed timetable," to sex and relationship education days, to assemblies on staying safe online, to small group activities talking to primary aged children about how they use the Internet. All of these activities interlink and complement each other, which is why I chose to interact so richly with young people in their education settings—such interactions result in a far deeper evidence base than if one was to constrain the discussion to a number of discrete research questions which can sometimes result in curtailing discussions to return to the precise focus of a specific hypothesis or question.

As well as working with young people I often find that I am asked to work with adults, for example parents' sessions in schools talking about online safety, staff training looking at OFSTED guidance and how that related to practice in the classroom, and presentations and Q&A sessions with practitioners looking at the gulf between adults' perceptions on children safety and the reality of what it is like for young people to grow up in this digital world. As such, this ethnography allows for an immersive and rich experience and, while it seems facile to say it, one where I spend more time listening than I do talking. This in turn provides a very detailed "dataset" comprising transcripts, quotes and extensive field notes that illustrate the complexity of relationships in the online world and how interrelated all of these issues are. For example, while a parent may be concerned about the amount of time their child is spending on a game, we are actually exploring what it means to be a parent in a household where young people know more about technology and how authority can still be exerted while feeling vulnerable about challenging behaviour the parent doesn't understand. And when talking to young children about how their friend destroyed their village on Minecraft—which we might be doing in a humorous, light hearted manner—we are really exploring issues of respect, empathy and boundaries and what we view as unacceptable in the online world compared to the offline one, and at the same time challenging what we understand by "child online safety." Even with this simple example, the "prohibition model" of safety—where we assume the young person is a passive consumer of content and we look at how to prevent access to "harmful content"—fails: we are talking about an interaction between peers, and therefore need to address it in a very different way to the control of content access.

In addition to this observational evidence base, this exploration will draw on data from two large quantitative datasets so we can baseline practice in schools around online safety and also young people's engagement with online technologies and their attitudes toward safety. The 360 Degree Safe tool (Phippen 2010), which will be discussed in more detail in Chap. 6, is an online safety self-review tool for schools which allows them to measure their own online safety performance across a range of metrics. Now used by over 8000 schools in the UK, the database behind the tool allows us to explore national performance, look at strengths and weaknesses, regional variation, and so on. In the context of this book it allows us to explore the "state of the nation" as far as schools online safety policy and practice is concerned, and compare this with where national policy lies. The second large dataset draws on survey data conducted by the South West Grid for Learning (http://www.swgfl.org.uk/), an online safety charity which conducts a survey with the schools they visit and which allows them to gauge the use of technology by young people so they can personalise training or education provision. At the time of writing, that survey has collected responses from over 13,000 children and young people across the country and, while not complex in its breadth, it does allow some fundamental questions about children's digital lives to be answered which, again, help contribute to the broader evidence base around keeping young people safe online.

A final aspect to raise at the start of this text, which we will return to later, draws from one of the Byron Review recommendations to move the discussion around online safety away from "media 'causing' harm to one which focuses on children and young people." In my experience of living in this space for the last five years, probably one of the weakest voices in the whole debate is that of the young people themselves. In another discussion with a teenager I was working with last year, who was doing a piece of work herself on the influence of digital technology on body image, she said this:

> When telling some of my friends and family about this project, one of the things I constantly found myself saying is that I want people to properly understand what teenagers are experiencing.

What I think is particularly telling from that statement is that she was talking about what teenagers are *experiencing*. While we, as policy makers, academics and practitioners within the community, try to address issues arising from our own concerns, and from public and media opinion, with preconceived ideas about what it is like for young people to grow up in this connected, complex world, none of us are experiencing it. Young people are, and they have a right to be heard as well as a right to be protected.

Drawing a rights-based perspective, particularly focusing on the UN Convention on the Rights of the Child (UN General Assembly 1989), is a useful tool in placing a framework around our understanding of child online safety. In the early chapters of this book I will propose the need for a policy approach that incorporates, rather than restricts, the rights of young people to engage with digital technology, whether this is voluntarily (e.g. through social communication, gaming and entertaining, content creation) or as a requirement (e.g. within school systems).

In delving into all of what has been discussed above in more detail, this book will be broken into a number of interlinked chapters that will develop themes, present evidence and challenge thinking on what it means to keep children safe online. In the early chapters of the book we will look in more detail at both public opinion and policy response, so as to frame the thinking in this space and highlight the potential challenges of these approaches, particularly from a rights-based perspective. The early chapters will also explore the UN Convention on the Rights of the Child in more detail once we have developed a clearer picture of public and government opinion in this area, to show the erosion of children's rights that occurs with a prohibitive approach to safety.

Once we have established these positions, we will explore the evidence base in more detail to highlight flaws in the existing policy positions. Firstly we will conduct a broad examination of the quantitative datasets mentioned above to allow a "baseline" of grass roots activity. Then we will start to challenge some of the thinking around risk and harm to young people online. In developing these issues further, two specific, often misunderstood digital phenomena, will be explored in depth. The first of these, sexting, or the exchange of sexually explicit messages and images using mobile and digital devices, is something that has caused much interest in the media, and much political debate. However, what is discussed far less is the broader context of sexting—why it happens, what are the wider cultural influences around it, and how it relates to other "online safety" related issues.

The second detailed exploration will be around gaming—often discussed but usually, once again, with an entirely content-based focus. In Chap. 4, gaming will be discussed, not just as a pastime, but as a sub-culture within some young people's lives. Rather than just focusing on how content impacts upon them, the chapter will look broadly at the issues that arise through being a gamer.

In drawing on this rich evidence base, the rest of the book will return to, and challenge, the policy perspectives to date, and argue that reactive policy forming is failing young people and denying them their fundamental rights. It will also refocus what we understand by child online safety, and propose the need for a more inclusive approach to understanding how young people engage with technology and how we, as a society, might consider how to ensure they can live their lives while remaining safe and free from harm.

CHAPTER 2

Public Concern and the Policy "Solution"

Abstract The media representation of the use of digital technology by children can be a skewed one, with an emphasis on negative "human interest" stories, perhaps as a result of positive stories doing little to sell news products. However, the author argues that such a media focus has resulted in both public interest and policy direction converging upon the narrow media discourse around access to pornography. Evidence is provided through an analysis of the policy approaches from the last UK coalition government over the previous five years, albeit using the earlier Byron Review as a starting point. The author suggests that the policy focus has been in an extremely narrow aspect of online safety—access to inappropriate content, more specifically pornography—with the sole solution being to address the need for technology such as blocking and filtering. He proposes that prohibitive approaches will do little to address the concerns raised and suggests that, rather than empowering young people, such approaches can have a serious impact upon children's rights.

Keywords Child online safety · Policy · UK government · Media · Safeguarding · Filtering · Pornography · Children's rights

This chapter will explore public concerns around online safety and where they come from, arguing that this is the foundation of the policy responses that have followed. The vast majority of policy discussion in the UK over

© The Author(s) 2017
A. Phippen, *Children's Online Behaviour and Safety*,
DOI 10.1057/978-1-137-57095-6_2

the last five years has been around access to pornography by younger children and its potential impact.

The approach gained a lot of support from some parts of the UK press, with headlines such as "Children grow up addicted to online porn sites: Third of 10-year-olds have seen explicit images" (Daily Mail 2012b) demanding that service providers "do more." This view is very direct and simple—service providers are facilitating access to such content, therefore they should stop it. It also takes another clear position—we understand the impact of pornography on young people and it is negative and damaging.

In exploring this policy position, this chapter will review the evolution of this thinking, initially looking at the post-Byron Review (Byron 2008) recommendations and responses (such as the formation of the UK Council for Child Internet Safety) before exploring key developments during the current parliament and also bringing in further initiatives that have emerged during the writing of this book (October 2015—February 2016). The 2010–2015 period is deliberately chosen as it represents the years in which the UK Conservative/Liberal Democrat coalition was in power, so we have a period of political stability. It is also interesting to use this period since it was during this time that the Byron Review was commissioned, took place and was subsequently deployed by the previous government.

In exploring the major policy developments during this time this chapter will present an argument that these have been driven not from an effective evidence base, but from media pressure and "quick wins" that focussed on a particularly high profile and salacious aspect of child online safety, and that failed to explore more long term, complex needs, even though these requirements were described in the Byron Review.

The term "policy" is used deliberately to encapsulate not just legislative change but also regulatory change, political pressure on industry and the nature of parliamentary debate. Drawing from significant personal experiences in providing evidence to Parliamentary inquiries, presentations at Westminster events and meetings with policy advisors and Members of Parliament, I will explore the sorts of issues the process was trying to tackle, the understanding of young people's online behaviours and how to address the social concerns that arise, as well as the motivations to address these.

I will then begin to unpick the issues that have been tackled and propose how such approaches might present challenges rather than solutions. I will explore the policy approaches against a framework of children's rights and suggest that, if we fail to understand the wider context around what "child online safety" actually is, the policies and subsequent actions will fail to provide solutions to the problems they propose to address.

THE POST-BYRON REVIEW PERIOD

Following the publication of the Byron Review, published in 2008, and discussed in Chap. 1, the government of the day responded with a number of commitments based on the recommendation of the review (UK Government 2009):

- The establishment of the UK Council for Child Internet Safety;
- Better regulation and the development of a self-regulation approach for industry;
- A commitment to public-awareness raising of online safety issues;
- A commitment to establishing "better education" for children and young people;
- Reformation of the classification of video games;
- Working with industry to improve information and support to parents on video games.

It is important to note that a lot of these recommendations focussed on the protection from harmful content. This is not surprising given the initial remit of the review was to look at how to protect young people from "potentially harmful and inappropriate content."

Two years after these commitments were published, Professor Byron released an "update" report, which was largely positive about how things had moved forward, drawing largely on the establishment of the UK Council for Child Internet Safety, and how that council was working with government to deliver on commitment. However, it was somewhat critical of the media's role in public awareness, stating that its focus remained largely on high profile tragedies and negative reporting of the influence of online technology on young people's lives:

> Since my 2008 review there has been increased media debate around this issue, which can helpfully embed it within societal consciousness. However, I do believe that the reporting of these issues still predominantly focuses on the extreme, often tragic, and thankfully rare cases of harm to children and

young people. I urge those reporting on these issues to take a proportionate and balanced view to ensure that they represent the needs of all children and young people who engage with the digital world (Byron 2010).

The Role of the Media as a Stakeholder in Child Online Safety

Moving into the period of study (2010 to 2015) the comment regarding the media from Professor Byron certainly resonates with my own experiences. To be fair to journalists and media outlets, it is the nature of their business that they need to have attention grabbing headlines in order to encourage sales of their products. However, if we draw from the two most popular newspapers in the UK—the *Daily Mail* and *The Sun*, who have a combined readership of over 2.5 million—we can see a generally negative theme across a lot of the reporting on issues related to children and online technology (Table 2.1).

My own work has been reported on in more than one of the headlines above. My experiences in talking to journalists about these issues is that there are *some* that wish to know about the in-depth issues and report on them in a manner that reflects the complexities of the relationships between young people and technology. However, these articles rarely make the front pages of newspapers, such as the two above. The other type of journalist I speak to has less interest in the complexities, they are more interested in basic statistics (e.g. "How many children sext?" "How many primary aged children are on social media?") or "human interest" angles—I have been asked on many occasions if I can put a journalist in touch with a "child who looks at pornography" or a "victim of sexting"; or, as happened in one case, "Have you got any really bad kids I can speak to?" Moreover, it is a rare interview where a journalist wishes to talk about the positive aspects of young people and their use of technology.

One might argue that it is not the role of the media to report on the complexities of a piece of research and that they need to engage the public with a human interest angle and base statistics to raise awareness—after all, more detailed dissemination will usually be found in reports or academic publications. However, the danger of a constant stream of sensational headlines is that a lack of balance means that policy makers respond to the extreme, rather than the norm.

Table 2.1 Sample of UK newspaper headlines related to children and technology

Headline	URL
Children grow up addicted to online porn sites: Third of 10-year-olds have seen explicit images	www.dailymail.co.uk/news/article-2131799/Children-grow-addicted-online-porn-sites-Third-10-year-olds-seen-explicit-images.html#ixzz40vXxKDDw
So, Minister, since when were the civil liberties of porn users more important than those of children?	www.dailymail.co.uk/debate/article-2133640/So-Minister-civil-liberties-porn-users-important-children.html#ixzz40vYDJgec
Schools minister backs explicit sex education for children aged 11: Education Secretary Nicky Morgan gives green light to controversial resource providing schoolchildren with information about pornography and rape	www.dailymail.co.uk/news/article-2771618/Schools-minister-backs-explicit-sex-education-children-aged-11-Education-Secretary-Nicky-Morgan-gives-green-light-controversial-resource-providing-schoolchildren-information-pornography-rape.html#ixzz40vZCUyx4
Sexting "is just a part of growing up" say new guidelines as police are told to avoid "draconian" prosecutions of teenagers that could harm their futures	www.dailymail.co.uk/news/article-3447313/Sexting-just-growing-say-new-guidelines-police-told-avoid-draconian-prosecutions-teenagers-harm-futures.html#ixzz40va3jll6
Sex texts epidemic: Experts warn sharing explicit photos is corrupting children	www.dailymail.co.uk/news/article-2246154/Sex-texts-epidemic-Experts-warn-sharing-explicit-photos-corrupting-children.html#ixzz40vaNmZsm
Schoolgirl is "trolled to death": Parents' agony as daughter, 14, "hangs herself" after horrific abuse from bullies on website Ask.fm	www.dailymail.co.uk/news/article-2384866/Schoolgirl-Hannah-Smith-trolled-death-bullies-Ask-fm-website.html#ixzz40vdkV3Iv
Violent video games DO trigger aggressive behaviour, decade-long review claims	www.dailymail.co.uk/sciencetech/article-3201001/Violent-video-games-trigger-aggressive-behaviour-decade-long-review-claims.html#ixzz40vaqwpfK
Furious dad bans all video games after son accidentally spends £4,000 playing FIFA	www.thesun.co.uk/sol/homepage/features/6858896/Furious-dad-bans-all-video-games-after-son-accidentally-spends-4000-playing-FIFA.html
Study shows exam grades plummet for teen gamers	www.thesun.co.uk/sol/homepage/features/6687648/Study-shows-exam-grades-plummet-for-teen-gamers.html

Table 2.1 (continued)

Headline	URL
Kids of 6 and 7 quizzed over phone sext pics	www.thesun.co.uk/sol/homepage/news/6628826/Kids-of-6-7-quizzed-over-phone-sext-pics.html
Kids who "sext" could end up being prosecuted	www.thesun.co.uk/sol/homepage/news/5776042/kids-who-sext-could-end-up-being-prosecuted.html
Staggering number of young children are viewing porn as Government launches major crackdown	www.thesun.co.uk/sol/homepage/news/politics/6934353/Staggering-number-of-young-children-are-viewing-porn-as-Government-launches-major-crackdown.html
"Parents to blame" for underage use of Facebook: Social media network admits it is powerless to stop children signing up	www.dailymail.co.uk/news/article-2267184/Experts-blame-parents-underage-use-Facebook-admits-powerless-stop-young-children-signing-up.html#ixzz40veEbPWh

Note: URLs accessed 1 May 2016

THE ALL PARTY INQUIRY INTO CHILD ONLINE SAFETY

Perhaps the first major policy activity of this government was the All Party Inquiry into Child Online Safety (Perry 2012), which ran from 2011 to 2012, and was chaired by Claire Perry MP. The inquiry began with a clear focus on early exposure of young people to pornography and strongly argued for the need for home filtering to ensure child safety. The inquiry was also clear that the main focus of responsibility for this lay with Internet service providers (ISPs)—the view being they were the ones who provided homes with access to the Internet, therefore they should be the ones to ensure responsible delivery of content. The final report of the inquiry drew a number of clear recommendations:

- The panel concluded that children have far too easy access to pornography and that it has a negative impact on their lives. It also noted that we should be concerned about other content such as hate speech, self-harm and pro-anorexia sites.
- ISPs make considerable revenue from providing Internet access and need to do more to ensure homes can prevent inappropriate content

from being accessed by children. ISPs need to provide parents with an "active choice" to install filters in the home to prevent this.

- ISPs and others in the "supply chain" should be doing more to provide parents with easy to access information around online safety.
- Network level filtering would be the "ideal" as it would mean that filtering could be provided for all devices in a home and managed by the ISP. There were technical reasons why this was not really possible at the time of the inquiry, though it was clear that this was viewed as an ideal position. However, the inquiry did acknowledge that "no filtering system will ever deliver total protection and parents will still need to remain engaged and active in helping their families stay safe online."
- The panel stated that at the present time self-regulation was more positive than legislation; however, if ISPs persisted with "ideological opposition" then legal provision may be needed.

In my own experience of the inquiry, as someone who was both called to give oral evidence and a written submission, I found the focus extremely narrow—almost entirely focussed on access to pornography, which seemed to conflict with my experience and conversations with children, education professionals and online safety practitioners around what was needed at a national level. Within the inquiry questioning itself, the challenge from the panel seemed to be that if you did not support their aims you wanted children to see pornography. It seemed not to acknowledge that technical measures might not actually work, that failings of filters in terms of over-blocking were not explored in depth, or that, if contributors were opposed to such proposals, it was not because they did not support the aim of managing access to pornography for children, but that they knew this approach would not work and would have potential detrimental impacts on children's rights.

Following this inquiry, and subsequent dialogue with ISPs, the "default opt in" option for home filtering began to become common place,[1] alongside other measures such as the filtering of public wifi hotspots.[2] Again, this seemed on the one hand perfectly reasonable—after all, no one wishes to sit in a cafe while someone on the opposite table is "enjoying" pornography—but on the other hand, if the aim was "child online safety" then was it addressing a real problem? In my own experience, and in discussion with young people, it seemed unlikely that public spaces were used to access and download pornography, or, as I was quoted in one Westminster event, "cracking one off in Starbucks" (Clarke 2014).

David Cameron's Speech on Child Online Safety at the NSPCC, July 2013

Another major policy activity following the Inquiry was a speech delivered by David Cameron, the UK Prime Minister, at the offices of the National Society for the Prevention of Cruelty to Children (Cameron 2013), on the subject of "Online Child Safety." Once again this speech focussed on young people's access to harmful content and what the government would do to prevent this, opening with the comment:

> The fact is that the growth of the internet as an unregulated space has thrown up two major challenges when it comes to protecting our children. The first challenge is criminal and that is the proliferation and accessibility of child abuse images on the internet. The second challenge is cultural; the fact that many children are viewing online pornography and other damaging material at a very early age and that the nature of that pornography is so extreme it is distorting their view of sex and relationships.

> And today, after months of negotiation, we've agreed home network filters that are the best of both worlds. By the end of this year, when someone sets up a new broadband account, the settings to install family friendly filters will be automatically selected; if you just click next or enter, then the filters are automatically on.

By December 2013, an agreement between the government and the four ISPs, under which they committed to offering all new customers a family-friendly network level filtering service, was announced (in the face of a threat to ISPs that if they didn't do something voluntarily, the government would legislate). There was much debate around the "default on" for such filters, meaning that a new subscriber would have to switch off filters actively on installation, rather than having to make the choice to have them installed. In the end a compromise of "active choice" was proposed, where the filter wouldn't be switched on without a confirmation from the end user. However, ISPs were free to "encourage" an opt in.

The speech was, once again, extremely narrow in its definition of online safety, suggesting that the key issue in protecting children online is in ensuring they do not get access to pornography. This speech extended that by saying that access to child abuse images is also a danger for children. What was very clear from the speech was that the ISPs were not providing the "solution."

David Cameron's Follow-up Speech in December 2014 at WeProtect

Following on from July 2013, the Prime Minister gave another speech at WeProtect in December 2014 (Cameron 2014). While this was purported to be an "update" on the July 2013 speech, the focus was entirely on child abuse images, rather than on online safety as a whole. However, while the focus of the speech is beyond the scope of this text, it is worth drawing on parts of it, which looks at the control of access to child abuse images through technical means:

> First, blocking search results. Until recently, it was incredibly easy for people to search the internet for child abuse and get results. And even sometimes have their search terms automatically completed for them. It was appalling. And yet, when we talked about changing it, a lot of people said, "Can't be done. You can't police the internet. You can't infringe internet freedoms in any way." But we said you can't have the freedom to search for vile material trumping a child's freedom to have an innocent childhood. So I made very clear the industry would have to find a way to block these search results and if they didn't then we would look at legislation.

> And I'm glad to say it hasn't come to that. In fact, internet companies have gone above and beyond what we asked of them. 95 % of online searches are processed by Google and Microsoft, and these companies have led the way. They stopped the autocomplete technology from finishing the search terms of those looking for child abuse. They then came up with new algorithms to block illegal images and videos. And Google now apply this to searches made in 40 different languages, so automatically checking against millions of search terms every single day.

> Microsoft are increasing the size of their blacklist to tens of thousands of terms, none of which will return any child abuse results at all. When people do search for this, they're confronted with pages warning them off, telling them they're breaking the law. And because it's getting harder to look for this material, Google have seen a fivefold reduction in these searches over the last year. So I think these are big steps forward. They're proving that the internet doesn't have to be a place that is beyond the pale or beyond the law. And I want to thank the internet companies for making this happen.

So with this detail from the speech, we can see a number of technical counter-measures to control the searching of indecent images of children. There are a number of issues pertinent to my arguments that can be drawn from this:

1. The focus, once again, is on industry to "do more," with the threat of legislation if they do not.
2. The main search engines have come up with technical measures to prevent the retrieval of results that would return indecent images of children.
3. A number of search terms have been "blacklisted" which result in a page alerting searchers that the material they are searching for is illegal.

There seems to have been some success with this, such that Google have seen a large reduction in searches on these keywords (Al-Riyami 2015). And once again, this is viewed as a significant victory for "child safety." However, one might argue that, as occurred in the case of the "right to be forgotten" legislation (Rosen 2012), this approach does nothing to remove the material, just the index to that material; and though it makes it more difficult to find, it is still online if one wishes to look for it via other means, such as image lockers, peer to peer systems and similar.

Regardless of the numerous technical issues around approaches to "stamping out" access to child sexual abuse images, we should also reflect on the prohibitive ideology. The view seems to be that, if one cannot access such materials, the problem will go away. A recent study by the UK-based Internet Watch Foundation (IWF) (Internet Watch Foundation 2015), however, shows that access to, and hosting of, this material is not being stamped out at all.

This research showed that 17.5 %of the 3803 sexually explicit, "self-generated" photos and videos analysed by the IWF (who had powers, for the first time, to search proactively for such content without risk of prosecution) depicted young people believed to be under the age of 15, while 7.5 % were assessed as including children aged 10 and younger. Even more startling was the severity of the content: just under half of the images of children aged 15 and under saw the subjects engaged in highly graphic sexual displays. However, most significantly was the fact that the majority of the material of minors was accessed not from websites, but from image hosts (e.g. websites that provide cloud based storage), which would not have been indexed by search engines and therefore could not be accessed through them. This demonstrates that search engines are only one route to such material.

While this is certainly both alarming and concerning, it highlights that, while political rhetoric is demanding such content be removed from the Internet, and speeches like the one above claims great strides forward, the material is still out there, the forms of production are becoming more varied and complex, and the modes of access continue to be diverse.

European Court of Justice Ruling on the Legality of Filtering

On 27 October 2015 the European Court of Justice (ECJ) ruled in the *Scarlet Extended (Belgacom Group)* v. *Sabam* case (Billington 2015) that requiring ISPs to use systems "for filtering and blocking electronic communications is inconsistent with EU law." This case hinged on an injunction on a Belgian ISP that attempted to force it to filter content to protect the copyright of the creators and ensure illegal downloads could not take place. However, the ruling stated that ISPs "can't be made to install monitoring systems to prevent illegal downloads of copyrighted material" as that would result in a monitoring of content on their networks which would contravene Article 15(1) of the E-Commerce Directive:

> Member States shall not impose a general obligation on providers, when providing the services covered by Articles 12, 13 and 14, to monitor the information which they transmit or store, nor a general obligation actively to seek facts or circumstances indicating illegal activity. (European Union 2000)

In going further, and reflecting from a rights perspective we will return to later, the ruling also stated that such monitoring would also "infringe the fundamental rights of the ISP's customers, namely their freedom to receive or impart information and their right to protection of their personal data"; that content must be allowed to travel across Internet infrastructure "without discrimination, restriction or interference."

This ruling would suggest that measures resulting from the policy development discussed above, with ISPs pressured to filter content delivered to their subscribers' homes, in order to address concerns by the UK government around children accessing "inappropriate" content, would also be unlawful.

Clearly this presented the prohibitive policy direction around child online safety with a challenge in EU law. However, such was the government's focus on filtering as the solution to the protection of children from access to content such as pornography, it was soon announced that they would be looking to change the legislation to ensure that such a ruling was not applicable in the UK. Speaking in the House of Commons on 28 October 2015 at Prime Minister's Questions,[3] Amanda Solloway MP asked:

> Yesterday, the EU said that we can no longer have internet filters to protect our children from indecent images. I want to know what the Prime Minister will do to ensure that our children remain protected.

Mr Cameron stated:

> Like my hon. Friend, I think that it is vital that we enable parents to have that protection for their children from this material on the internet. Probably like her, I spluttered over my cornflakes when I read the *Daily Mail* this morning, because we have worked so hard to put in place those filters. I can reassure her on this matter, because we secured an opt-out yesterday so that we can keep our family-friendly filters to protect children. I can tell the House that we will legislate to put our agreement with internet companies on this issue into the law of the land so that our children will be protected.

As a result of this ruling, the opt-out places in the UK are at odds with the rest of Europe on this matter. However, more concerning is the promise of further legislation to enshrine the need for ISPs to filter content in law, even though the ECJ ruling made it clear that there were both issues related to legality in EU law, and also the control of Internet content from a rights perspective (potentially at odds with human rights as defined by the UN). This seems to contradict an earlier agreement with service providers that if they were proactive they would not be legislated. It now seems, even though ISPs did respond, the legislation will be enacted.

Baroness Howe's Online Safety Bill

A further step toward legislation can be seen in a bill currently being discussed in the House of Lords, Baroness Howe's Online Safety bill (UK Parliament 2016), which is:

A Bill to make provision about the promotion of online safety:

- to require internet service providers and mobile phone operators to provide an internet service that excludes adult content;
- to require electronic device manufacturers to provide a means of filtering internet content;
- to make provision for parents to be educated about online safety and for the regulation of harmful material through on-demand programme services.

So, once again, we have a policy instrument that is proposing online safety while focussing on forcing industry to provide filters to exclude pornography. However, it does also place a focus on parental/public education, albeit driven from industry. In exploring the bill in more detail, a couple of key aspects can be drawn from the document:

Section 3:
Internet service providers and mobile telephone operators must provide prominent, easily accessible and clear information about online safety to customers at the time the internet service or mobile telephone is purchased and shall make such information available for the duration of the service.
Section 4:
The Secretary of State must provide means of educating parents of children under the age of 18 about:

(a) the exclusion of adult content from an internet access service under section 1 to protect children;
(b) additional online safety measures for electronic devices, including but not restricted to, age appropriate filters; and
(c) protecting their child from online behaviour that could be a safety risk, including but not restricted to bullying and sexual grooming.

So while the focus in section 3 is on industry providing clear information on safety, section 4 is also, encouragingly, looking to the Secretary of State to provide parental education, firstly related to content control/ filtering, but then, as can be seen in part (c), to "online behaviour that could be a safety risk." This seems to move from a highly focussed requirement for education to an extremely broad one in the space of a few statements. It is important, therefore, to understand what the thinking behind the bill believes online safety to be, which it defined as "the safe and responsible use of the internet by children and young people on an electronic device."

This is a broad but vague definition that would benefit from further exploration and discussion. The only debate over the bill in the House of Lords seemed to avoid the issue of education or what online safety "is." The debate included contributions by Baroness Shields, the Minister for Internet Safety and Security:

> Baroness Shields—comment from Hansard on 11/12/2015 debate:
> However, as my noble friends and colleagues have mentioned, there is always more that can be done, and no filters or technological tools will be 100% successful all the time. It is crucial that parents continue to engage with their children's internet experiences and ensure that they build awareness of and resilience to things they see on the internet which may upset them or cause them harm. It is also vital that we, as the Government, continue our effective and productive relationships with industry and Ofcom to consider how our world-class internet safety protections can be made even better.

This comment is particularly interesting because it acknowledges that a total reliance on technology will not succeed, and there needs to be other factors in achieving "online safety," in particular returning to the need for parental awareness, and engagement.

However, others in the debate seemed further focussed on the essential nature of filtering to address the problems:

> Baroness Benjamin—comment from Hansard on 11/12/2015 debate:
> My Lords, this is a probing amendment and I very much look forward to hearing what the Minister says in response. Following the net neutrality vote in Brussels, it would seem that if the filtering arrangements negotiated by the Prime Minister—I congratulate him on them—are to continue, the Government must bring forward legislation to make them a reality by April.

On the confusion regarding the filters regime and its legality in terms of Europe, we must legislate to make our filters regime legal according to the new net neutrality regulations. The date for that is by December 2016. To be clear: we need to do something to keep our existing regime viable and functional under the law.

Again, this raises the issue that even legislative challenge to the legal implications of controlling Internet access and content should be disregarded because the filtering solution is correct, and anyone who disagrees with it is wrong. Moreover, this comment reflects the urgency of putting legislation in place to enforce filtering, even though the major service providers had already voluntarily agreed to make filters available to subscribers.

However, perhaps what was most concerning, when analysing the discourse in the transcript, was that there was not a single mention of education, let alone effective education provision for children. It showed once again that children were viewed as passive stakeholders in their relationship with the digital world, where they have to have safety foisted upon them, rather than having positive engagement with it themselves.

Consultation of Safeguarding in School, January 2016

In January 2016 the Department for Education launched a consultation of new safeguarding guidelines in schools, which included draft statutory guidance (Department for Education 2015a). While much of this consultation lies outside of the scope of this there are some interesting points that highlight both some positive and concerning attitudes toward what online safety should be in schools:

75. As schools and colleges increasingly work online it is essential that children are safeguarded from potentially harmful and inappropriate online material. As such governing bodies and proprietors should ensure appropriate filters and appropriate monitoring systems are in place. Children should not be able to access harmful or inappropriate material from the school or college's IT system. Governing bodies and proprietors should be confident that systems are in place that will identify children accessing or trying to access harmful and inappropriate content online.

It is interesting to note that within this section of the draft guidance, monitoring systems are beginning to be discussed, alongside filtering. Filtering has been used in schools for a considerable length of time and is a well established piece of technology for controlling access to inappropriate material; however, even as far back as the Byron Review concern was raised around over-reliance on filtering as the solution to online safety issues in school. Monitoring, on the other hand, is a more recent addition to safeguarding in schools and, while it can be a useful tool, we also have to be mindful that it can place restrictions on individuals' privacy rights, particularly when put in place with little concern for transparency or data protection.

The concern with this draft guidance is that, while monitoring is now placed as an expectation of the governing body, there is little to say the same body is also responsible for the data collected by such systems and is mindful of the rights to the privacy of individuals. The concern is that, again, a technical system is being viewed as something to provide a solution to a problem with a social context. In the launch document for the consultation (Department for Education 2015b), it is stated:

All schools will:

- Need to have appropriate filters and monitoring systems, so that no child can access harmful content via the school's IT systems and concerns can be spotted quickly;
- Be required to ensure that they teach their pupils about safeguarding, including online.

This suggests that, with monitoring in place, concerns can quickly be identified and addressed.

What is missing from this guidance is advice around privacy of the child and the requirement for consent for the collection, use and storage of a child's data. Clearly their browsing habits and communications using school systems would be covered by this. The schools would also have a responsibility to ensure that the data was protected and that appropriate security around these systems was in place.

While monitoring systems can be used to intercept abuse and harassment, we have also to be mindful about where information is disclosed in an area where personal prejudice might result in risk to the individual being monitored. For example, if a child is identified as trying to access an LGBT website through a monitoring system, who would see this information, and what would be done about it (given that an alert around access to a blocked site had been raised)? There are issues around transparency that are not dealt with whatsoever in this document, and one would hope these will be raised within the consultation.

> 77. Governing bodies and proprietors should ensure children are taught about safeguarding, including online, through teaching and learning opportunities, as part of providing a broad and balanced curriculum. This may include covering relevant issues through personal, social health and economic education (PSHE), and/or—for maintained schools and colleges—through sex and relationship education (SRE).

It is encouraging to see that safeguarding education, including online issues, is expected to be delivered in schools. However, guidance on where it should be delivered, and how, and what should be covered, are all lacking. And the suggestion of placing it within PSHE or SRE is welcomed, although given the Secretary of State for Education's response to calls by the Education Select Committee to make PSHE/SRE compulsory in schools, as discussed below, would suggest that the level and quality of education around this topic will remain patchy at best (this will be discussed in far more detail in Chap. 6).

> 78. Whilst it is essential that governing bodies and proprietors ensure that appropriate filters and monitoring systems are in place; they should be careful that "over blocking" does not lead to unreasonable restrictions as to what children can be taught with regards to online teaching and safeguarding.

It is good to see that over-blocking is finally being acknowledged as an issue caused by filtering, which would also prevent access to much material around SRE and online issues such as pornography and sexting. However, bearing in mind this is draft *statutory* guidance, the implication here is that governing bodies at schools are responsible to ensure over-blocking does not happen on their premises. As will be discussed in Chap. 5, governing bodies rarely receive training in these topics and, as raised above, such issues can have complex implications in terms of education, data protection and privacy.

As will be discussed in Chaps. 3 to 6 the view of young people increasingly appears to be that these issues need to fit into the "social education" part of the curriculum. I was speaking to a group of teenagers as part of a workshop on online privacy and identity recently and said that I was travelling to London the day afterwards to speak to a politician about these issues, and asked whether they wanted me to pass on anything for them. Two responses stand out from the young people:

1. "Tell them they could take all of the pornography in the world and bury it on a desert island, I'll still find it."
2. "Tell them to give us better sex education."

While the first comment was delivered in a somewhat sarcastic manner, the individual subsequently qualified it in a very mature manner by explaining that if the government felt that controlling access to pornography through filtering was a good idea, they were doomed to fail as there were too many other ways to access such content.

The second comment I found more interesting—we had not been talking about anything specifically around sexual behaviours (although the issue of filtering in schools had arisen, hence some discussion around their effectiveness), yet this young person, from a year 10 class, had clearly associated online behaviours with sexual and social education, rather than computing or information and computing technology.

If we explore national policy around PSHE and SRE, we see little activity over recent years. However, the Education Select Committee did carry out a consultation during 2014 around this provision in schools.

PSHE and SRE in Schools

The committee announced this inquiry in April 2014 (Education Select Committee 2014), with the following points to be addressed:

- Whether PSHE ought to be statutory, either as part of the National Curriculum or through some other means of entitlement.
- Whether the current accountability system is sufficient to ensure that schools focus on PSHE.
- The overall provision of SRE in schools and the quality of its teaching, including in primary schools and academies.
- Whether recent government steps to supplement the guidance on teaching about sex and relationships, including consent, abuse between teenagers and cyber-bullying, are adequate.
- How the effectiveness of SRE should be measured.

The inquiry took place in the wake of the House of Lords rejection of compulsory SRE earlier in that year. It was interesting to note that in the inquiry cyber-bullying and sexting were both raised as aspects of personal and social development that needed to be explored within curricula. In the summary of the report (Education Select Committee 2015) produced by the committee, they drew the following conclusion on the state of PSHE and SRE in schools:

> There is a lack of clarity on the status of the subject. This must change, and we accept the argument that statutory status is needed for PSHE, with sex and relationships education as a core part of it. We recommend that the Department for Education develops a work plan for introducing age-appropriate PSHE and SRE as statutory subjects in primary and secondary schools, setting out its strategy for improving the supply of teachers able to deliver this subject and a time table for achieving this. The statutory requirement should have minimal prescription content to ensure that schools have flexibility to respond to local needs and priorities. SRE should be renamed relationships and sex education to emphasise a focus on relationships.

> Parental engagement is key to maximising the benefits of SRE. The Government should require schools to consult parents about the provision of SRE, and ask Ofsted to inspect the way in which schools do this. The existing right of a parent to withdraw their child from elements of SRE must be retained.

The Government response to the inquiry report took some time; however, the Secretary of State for Education did write back to the inquiry chair, Neil Carmichael MP.

SECRETARY OF STATE FOR EDUCATION'S RESPONSE IN JANUARY 2016

Here is an excerpt from that letter (Morgan 2016):

> The vast majority of schools already make provision for PSHE and while the Government agrees that making PSHE statutory would give it equal status with other subjects, the Government is concerned that this would do little to tackle the most pressing problems with the subject, which are to do with the variable quality of its provision, as evidenced by Ofsted's finding that 40 % of PSHE teaching is less than good. As such, while we will continue to keep the

status of PSHE in the curriculum under review, our immediate focus will be on improving the quality of PSHE teaching in our schools.

I want PSHE to be at the heart of a whole-school ethos that is about developing the character of young people. I want it to be tailored to the individual needs of the school and for programmes to be based on the best available evidence of what works. I want senior leaders to ensure that it has the time in the curriculum and the status that it deserves within school and I want it to be taught by well-trained and well-supported staff.

What the response shows is that the government, at present, has little enthusiasm for the introduction of compulsory PSHE and SRE in schools, let alone to look in more detail at what the provision should be. The comment about 40 % of PSHE being less than good seems to be applying a bizarre logic—they are unwilling to look at compulsory delivery of the subject until the teaching in it is improved. Given the subject is not compulsory, one might suggest the reason why the teaching is less that good in some instances is that, without a statutory requirement for it to be delivered, senior leaders in schools would rather focus school improvement in other areas. This is something we will explore in later chapters, most specifically in Chap. 6.

A Prohibitive Approach to Child Online Safety

From the above discussion of policy developments over the last five years, we can see that the main focus on child online safety has been on the prevention of access to pornography. There has been very little focus on much else, and when the wider social education issues are raised, they are knocked back.

It seems that a prohibitive perspective on online safety is prevalent: if we ensure young people cannot access such content, they will be safe. I can recall being asked a question based very much on this notion during the Inquiry into Child Online Safety: "So if we can get this filtering cracked, we can solve these child online safety problems once and for all?" To which I replied: "No."

I qualified this negative response by explaining that we are actually looking at social issues raised by technology and that social issues can rarely be solved with technology alone. Even if we focus solely on pornography, the debate is a complex one and the research on its influence on children, and adults, is patchy at best. The recent, excellent review of the influence of pornography (Horvath et al. 2013) conducted for the UK's

Office of the Children's Commissioner came to a number of conclusions (e.g. that those who commit violent sexual assaults often have viewed violent pornography), but it also quite clearly stated there is a lot we still do not know (e.g. whether accessing violent pornography causes consumers to commit violent sexual acts).

From my own investigations I have obtained a similar picture. I will discuss young people's views on these matters throughout this text. An interesting illustration of the complexity of the evidence around the influence of pornography on young people can be drawn from the recent crime statistics related to the number of sexual crimes committed by minors over the last five years.

Last year, I placed a Freedom of Information access request to all police forces in England and Wales, with the intention of collecting clear statistics around sexual crimes committed by minors, in order to test the theory that, if young people are strongly negatively influenced by access to pornography, the growth in the easy availability of pornography over the last five years has a causal link with the number of such crimes.

The following Freedom of Information access request was sent to all England and Wales forces in April 2015:

Q1 Please could you provide the number of sexual offences (Home Office Offence Codes 16, 17, 17A, 17B, 18, 19A, 19B, 19C, 19D, 19E, 19F, 19G, 19H, 20, 20A, 20B, 21, 22, 22A, 22B, 23, 70, 71, 72, 73, 74, 88A, 88B, 88C, 88D, 88E) where the offender(s) are under the age of 18 for the years: 2010–2014.

Q2 Would it also be possible to provide the number of arrests for people under 18 related to the same sexual offence codes.

The results were collected subsequently over a number of weeks (with 38 forces returning results in total) and they present something that is far less conclusive than one might anticipate. What should be made clear from the outset is that, due to differences in reporting and data collection systems across forces, an overall aggregation of results was not carried out. However, each force was analysed based upon a linear regression of results over the five data points (in both cases, the value for the year divided by the five-year average made into a percentage), with the calculation of the regression coefficient indicating a negative (suggesting an on average reduction over time) or positive (suggesting an on average increase over time). The results are shown in Table 2.2.

Table 2.2   Positive and negative correlation counts from police force responses to Freedom of Information request

	Offences	*Arrests*[*]
Strongly positive (≥10)	9	4
Positive (≥0.5 and <10)	11	4
Level (<0.5 and >0.5)	2	2
Negative (≤−0.5 and >−10)	13	12
Strongly negative (≤−10)	3	13

*Three forces did not return arrest data

What the analysis shows is that, while in some forces there has been an increase in sexual offences committed by minors over the past five years, there is an almost equal number of forces in which they have decreased. In terms of arrests, there has been a decrease across 25 forces.

As with much data in this area, the results cannot be conclusive, nor would I wish for them to be considered as such. They cover a wide range of crime categories (from voyeurism and harassment to sexual assault and rape) and steer away from looking at specific criminal activity such as the number of rape charges against minors. Also, what is clear from my own work and that of others is that young people in a lot of cases do not recognise what we might view as "low level" sexual crimes (e.g. harassment), which therefore go unreported. Some young people, sadly, view such activities as part of everyday life, as illustrated in work such as Ringrose et al. (2012).

However, given the data presented, we cannot conclude that easier access to pornography has had a clear and straightforward impact on sexual crimes among minors. This is a complex area and finding, and proving, causal links is extremely difficult.

JOIN US, OR OPPOSE US

The other issue in this debate concerns the government perspective that suggests that you either support their plans or "want to let children see pornography"; this binary approach is not helpful. There are very few people in this field that would happily say that they don't believe pornography has any impact whatsoever on young people and that they should be free to access it.

In summary, the review of the current policy perspective, as mentioned above, is not intended as a criticism of Parliament and its attempts to address these complex issues. It is, however, further evidence that for some *content* is the key issue and prohibition is the solution. The fact is this was a policy approach looking to technology to solve a social problem. This is not to say that such approaches are not useful—certainly there is some benefit in putting technical countermeasures in place to prevent younger children from accidentally accessing content. However, issues around over-blocking and the bypassing of controls means that they do not even provide a solution to the content problems they are trying to address, particularly when extending the issues around content filtering beyond pornography to other forms of legal, but troubling, matter, such as hate speech, self-harm and gambling.

The Open Rights Group's project into blocking—Blocked.org (Open Rights Group 2016) showed that one in five websites was blocked by filters in their sample (none of which contained any harmful material—they included sexual health and education sites and politic fora). The home filters tested (which were the ones provided by the main ISPs) blocked much material that is actually designed to prevent harm—for example websites that offer advice about LGBT issues, sexual health, domestic violence, and drugs and alcohol. Given the expected level of filtering in schools, home is the only place that some children would have the opportunity to access such information safely.

In 2014, the UN Special Rapporteur's report on rights and freedom of expression (UN General Assembly 2014) stated:

> The result of vague and broad definitions of harmful information, for example in determining how to set Internet filters, can prevent children from gaining access to information that can support them to make informed choices, including honest, objective and age-appropriate information about issues such as sex education and drug use. This may exacerbate rather than diminish children's vulnerability to risks.

Returning to the issue of human rights resulting from the ECJ ruling discussed above, if we are to consider the potential impact of filtering children's rights, using the UN Convention on the Rights of the Children (UN General Assembly 1990) as our standard, we might specifically be contravening a number of articles that provide a framework for discussion of these rights as we progress through this text (Table 2.3).

Table 2.3   Children's rights from the UNCRC compared with prohibitive online safety measures

Article 12 (respect for the views of the child): when adults are making decisions that affect children, children have the right to say what they think should happen and have their opinions taken into account.	If we adopt a prohibitive approach to online safety, under the auspices of a need to ensure they avoid harm online, we are failing to incorporate the views of the child in this discussion—we are merely preventing them from accessing an aspect of online content. Without the provision of effective relationships and sexual education, young people do not get the opportunity to express their own views in this debate, or even ask questions.
Article 13 (freedom of expression): children have the right to get and share information, as long as the information is not damaging to them or others.	While we would not suggest that it is a child's right to access pornographic material, they should have a right to access information that is important to the social development of themselves, their peers, siblings. etc., e.g. issues of sexuality, sexual health, privacy, politics and rights. They may wish, e.g., to share information on sexuality with peers. We can evidence that Internet filters would prevent such things from being possible.
Article 16 (right to privacy): children have a right to privacy. The law should protect them from attacks against their way of life, their good name, their families and their homes.	If monitoring systems are being used, and seemingly increasingly so, there are potential implications for a young person's privacy which cannot be disregarded as such systems may help identify safeguarding concerns. Regardless of the use of such systems for safeguarding, their abuse can result in serious issues around privacy.
Article 17 (access to information; mass media): children have the right to get information that is important to their health and well-being.	Similarly to the comments around article 13, filtering will clearly block access to information around health and well-being, particular if that information is sexual in nature. However, they may also block valuable information on, e.g., self-harm, abuse and mental health.

Table 2.3 (continued)

Article 29 (goals of education): children's education should develop each child's personality, talents and abilities to the fullest. It should encourage children to respect others, human rights and their own and other cultures. It should also help them learn to live peacefully, protect the environment and respect other people.	With a prohibitive approach to SRE, we cannot expect a fully rounded development of the child on issues such as consent, empathy and respect. E.g., as is discussed in more detail in Chap. 4, the social context around sexting is less to do with the act of exchange of images, and more to do with the lack of understanding around boundaries and respect and self-esteem. Is it any wonder that young people engage in such practices with little awareness of these issues if they have never received education on such matters? While Article 29 has a broader reach than simply something complicated through filtering, we must also acknowledge that the government's legislative obsession around "online child protection" focuses almost entirely on the responsibilities of the ISP to ensure indecent content does not reach the young recipient, rather than considering the role of education in developing resilient young people who can deal with and cope with indecent content in an informed, mature manner.
Article 34 (sexual exploitation): governments should protect children from all forms of sexual exploitation and abuse. This provision in the Convention is augmented by the Optional Protocol on the sale of children, child prostitution and child pornography.	We might also argue that a lack of education on the matters discussed around Article 29 mean that children are more vulnerable to sexual exploitation. Discussed in more detail in Chap. 4, many young people find it difficult to appreciate that harassment via a mobile device is no less acceptable than harassment in person (see Ringrose 2012).
Article 42 (knowledge of rights): governments should make the Convention known to adults and children. Adults should help children learn about their rights, too. (See also article 4.)	An awareness of rights arises from effective social education, currently not part of the statutory curriculum in the UK. Given that digital technology can play a part in eroding rights (e.g. the right to privacy and the right to be free from harassment), I would argue that without effective social education which addresses these issues, we are failing children in this regard.

We will return to this framework once we have explored the evidence base around "child online safety" in more detail in the follow chapters. However, it is interesting to note that the Education Select Committee report also made specific reference to articles 17, 29 and 34.

Young people are very clear about where more effective approaches to addressing these issues should lie. What is still missing from the debate around legislation to protect against the harm of pornography is effective awareness and education. In my own experiences visiting schools and talking with young people about these issues I am struck by a number of points:

- An almost complete lack of awareness of the legal and rights based issues around protection from harassment, consent, freedom of speech, their own rights to education, privacy, etc.;
- An enthusiasm to engage in discussions around the topic, asking questions, across all manner of related issues (young people do not put these matters into boxes as many adults do);
- A desire for a common educational experience around these issues being shown in a video in assembly, rather than classroom discussion;
- A willingness to engage in further discussion/education around the topics, but for which no opportunity is provided.

I would ask whether the "solution" proposed by this policy direction is worth it? There seems to be a great deal of political rhetoric in the media about protecting children through these prohibitive approaches, but with little evidence to show that they are effective, or even used. In the recent OFCOM media literacy tracker (OFCOM 2014), a small minority of households had chosen to take up ISP offers to install home filtering.

Legislation that potentially impacts upon all of our human rights, with little evidence of providing a solution to the problems it claims to address, where we fail to have a clear understanding of the problems caused or the evidence base to support the policy direction, is something about which we should be extremely concerned. In addition, the focus entirely on one stakeholder in the complex relationships involved in online child safety and protection is doomed to fail. ISPs cannot provide the answers to this issue, as they can only, at best, restrict the delivery of content (although they may be breaking EU law if they do this). They can do nothing regarding the impact of such content if young people do seek it out and watch it. This is not to say that, because there is no conclusive proof, we should not be doing more to try to reduce access to such content and protect children from the potential harm that might arise from its viewing. However, the fact is pornography is part of the Internet and of course some young people look for it, no matter what technological countermeasures are put in place. However, they do believe they have a right to relationship and sexual education that is fit for purpose and relevant to the twenty-first century.

What is far less clear is whether a legislative approach with a singular focus on technological intervention is at all effective. The last five years of policy in this area has shown far more activity than has taken place in previous years, and this is indeed to be welcomed. But it remains a concern that proposing a solution that many can already demonstrate as ineffective, and then maintaining momentum on this route as a result of ideology rather than evidence while disregarding any concerns to the contrary, shows a somewhat blinkered, short term view to something that, as already discussed in Chap. 1, requires constant review and reflection due to changes in the technology, the behaviours and the legislation.

In subsequent chapters we will explore young people's relationships with digital technology in far more detail to evidence further why a prohibitive approach to online safety is ineffective at best and restrictive of human rights at worst. These chapters will draw extensively from primary data in exploring young people's relationship with technology to show that, rather than being passive consumers of other people's content, young people are dynamic, active engagers with the online world. It will become clear that there is an urgent need to address their lack of knowledge around risk taking behaviours and the impact of their actions online on others, along with complementary issues such as developing resilience, esteem and empathy. However, the approaches discussed in this chapter will not do any of these things.

Notes

1. For example https://sales.talktalk.co.uk/product/homesafe. Accessed 1 May 2016.
2. www.getmedigital.com/friendly-wifi. Accessed 1 May 2016.
3. www.publications.parliament.uk/pa/cm201516/cmhansrd/cm151028/debtext/151028-0001.htm#15102833000010. Accessed 30 January 2016.

CHAPTER 3

Young People and Digital Lives

Abstract The author stresses the importance of including the youth voice in any policy and subsequent legislative implementation around child online safety, given arguably that they are the citizens whose lives will be most impacted on by such approaches. Drawing from a large survey of young people he highlights that they, even at an early age, are not passive consumers of content but are actively engaged in all manner of social activity online. He expands on this perspective by showing that, from a young person's perspective, harm rarely comes from content and is actually drawn from a breadth of online environments where the main cause of upset online is not content, but people. As such, filtering and blocking solutions will rarely prevent this from happening. Through evidence as a result of discourse with young people the author raises concerns about preventative approaches to online safety and how a failure to tackle effectively such issues within education settings results in peer oriented resolutions to problems that arise.

Keywords Child online safety · Digital lives · Pornography · Filtering · Education

This chapter and the two following ones draw comparisons between policy direction and media focus on the one hand and grass-roots data with young people on the other. This suggests that young people are not

© The Author(s) 2017
A. Phippen, *Children's Online Behaviour and Safety*,
DOI 10.1057/978-1-137-57095-6_3

merely passive consumers and are in fact highly engaged with technology. I will highlight both the complexities of their relationships with technology and the gulf between what young people experience and how national policy aims to "protect" them. While Chaps 4 and 5 will look at particular "online phenomena" in order to explore specific issues in depth, this chapter will begin with a general discourse on young people and their online lives.

This exploration is driven in two ways. Firstly, in drawing on data from a large scale survey on young people's use of technology, we can establish some key points around their engagement with digital "lives," as well as looking at some age and gender differences. This will be developed considerably by drawing from many conversations (from formal interviews and focus groups, to informal dialogues in lessons, to Q&A sessions during assemblies and similar) with young people from the ages of 3 up to 18.

Secondly, we will explore young people's opinions around the key policy direction—specifically the control of access to harmful content. As a result of this, we will highlight the willingness of young people to talk about these issues, if, given the appropriate fora. We will also critique, from the perspective of young people, the quality of the education they receive.

The chapter concludes by suggesting that young people can have a very positive relationship with technology, that it does have the potential to distort social norms, and that, without a sound understanding of these issues, with a consistent and pragmatic educational approach, they can open themselves up to risk and harm. I also begin to argue that any "safety" based approach that aims to prevent either content access or unacceptable behaviour is missing the need of young people for education around this subject and which could lead to positive change.

YOUNG PEOPLE AND DIGITAL TECHNOLOGY

In commencing this exploration, we will "base line" young people's online lives through an exploration of a quantitative dataset. Following this, we will discuss the issues raised through this base lining against my many conversations with young people on these topics, hopefully highlighting the assertion of the chapter title—talking to young people about digital technology is a powerful way of understanding the issues they face and how we might help them.

The data we will initially explore is drawn from a survey run by the South West Grid for Learning,[1] an online safety charity which is a part of the UK Safer Internet Centre with considerable expertise in working in schools and the children's workforce on issues around online safety. The survey was developed in 2013 as a simple way of collecting basic data on the children from the schools the charity worked with. The survey was clear and straightforward in nature, collecting data around topics such as:

- Respondent demography (year group, gender);
- Technologies used to access the Internet and the sorts of things they used when online;
- Amount of time spent online;
- Whether they had ever received or engaged in hostile discourse online;
- Whether they had ever been upset by content online;
- Attitudes toward their online privacy;
- Who they turn to for support.

Since its inception, the survey has collected over 13,000 responses, which provides a very large dataset on young people's use of technology in the UK.

Obviously there are a number of other large surveys around young people's Internet use, EU Kids Online (Livingstone et al. 2011) and the OFCOM Media Literacy tracker (OFCOM 2011, 2014) being the most well known. The aim of this survey is not to replicate the complexity or detail of these pieces of work, but merely to draw some basic statistics on the use of technology by young people to underpin the subsequent ethnographic discussions.

Given the survey has been running for over three years now we will not explore the dataset as a whole—over three years Internet access has changed considerably (particularly with the advent of superfast broadband services across the UK) as have devices, services and behaviours. As such, we only draw on data for 2015—giving us a population of 5104 with a breakdown of year group as shown in Table 3.1.

The gender split in the population was almost perfectly even, with 51.4 % of respondents male and 48.6 % female. Therefore, with the

Table 3.1   Respondent year group

What year group are you in?

	Response (%)	*Response count*
Year 4	17.1	871
Year 5	18.5	945
Year 6	18.3	935
Year 7	13.2	673
Year 8	14.1	718
Year 9	9.0	461
Year 10	6.1	311
Year 11	3.7	190

Note: n = 5104

Table 3.2   Use of online technology

What do you use to go online? (please tick all you use)	*(%)*
Mobile/smart phone/other mobile device	64.77
Laptop/netbook	57.39
Tablet	67.59
Home gaming devices	42.75
Mobile gaming devices	21.22
Desktop PC	32.70
Television	34.82

Note: n = 5102

dataset we have a balanced gender representation, reflecting the broadly classroom-based data collection from the survey.

In Table 3.2 we can see the general use of technology for Internet access.

Table 3.2 highlights the significance of Internet access via mobile and portable technology, with tablet devices being the most popular, closely followed by mobile phones. We will return to this later in this chapter as technology use changes significantly over time.

From Table 3.3 it is clear that Internet access for the whole survey population plays a significant part in the respondents' lives, with the majority being online for at least an hour a day. For over 25 % of respondents, they spend more than three hours online.

In terms of what young people do online, Table 3.4 presents the first piece of data which starts to challenge the view of passive consumer.

Table 3.3 Time spent online

How much time do you spend online in an average day?	(%)
Less than an hour	32.5
One to three hours	41.2
Between three and six hours	17.3
More than six hours	9.0

Note: n = 4985

Table 3.4 Respondent online activities

What do you use the Internet for?	(%)
Social networks	44.08
Instant messaging, e.g. Windows Live, Skype, WhatsApp	39.76
Gaming	73.34
Shopping	30.89
News	20.90
Browsing/general entertainment	40.96
Listening to music	66.26
Uploading/content creation	31.58

Note: n = 4914

There are few surprises from these results—gaming being the most popular. While social media use may seem low, we should bear in mind that a significant proportion of the population is below the general age (13) for use of services such as Facebook, Instagram and Twitter.

However, we might note that the most significant, and perhaps surprising, result, especially for those who view young people's use of Internet technologies as a passive consumption, is the final one—uploading/ content creation. These are people who are creating their own content in some form (photo, video, etc.) and posting it online—the most popular service for this being YouTube. Almost a third of the population is engaged in content production online—they are engaging in the platforms, not just downloading content from them.

In developing this concept of online engagement, rather than consumption, we also asked whether respondents have ever been upset by things they had seen online, and what they were (Table 3.5).

Table 3.5   Being upset online

Have you ever seen anything on line that has made you feel upset?	*(%)*
Yes	29.4
No	70.6

Note: n = 4985

While the initial statistic shows that this population has clearly been affected/upset by things they had come across online, what was more interesting to explore were the sorts of things respondents said had upset them. We provided an open text question which followed the original question for respondents to elaborate on what had caused upset, and these responses provide a very detailed picture. For example:

- Swearing;
- People being mean;
- Videos and images of animal abuse;
- "Rude" content.

There is a lot of comment around abuse—people being aggressive or rude, or using offensive language. However, in terms of content, one thing that came up far more than any comments about pornographic images was animal abuse. This immediately presents a challenge if we are using a content prevention approach to "child protection"—how can we filter against this sort of thing, without preventing access to all manner of innocuous content about animals?

In addition, a number of comments fell into an area that we might refer to as purely social issues facilitated by digital technology which, consequently, cannot be solved through a preventative approach. To take a couple of specific comments to illustrate this:

- My friend texted me saying that her dad had died;
- When my dad told me on Facebook he didn't want to see me anymore.

In both of these cases no level of filtering or content control would have prevented these sort of things from happening—these are outcomes from

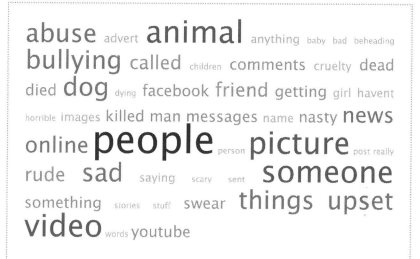

Fig. 3.1 Word cloud of responses around what causes upset online

the use of Internet technologies as a form of social interaction, rather than content consumption. In both cases it is clear that significant upset would have been caused, but it is challenging to consider any means of technical countermeasure that would prevent this sort of thing from happening.

Figure 3.1 shows a word cloud produced from all of the responses to this question.

It is interesting to note that by far the most prevalent term in all of the comments is "people." While "rude" does appear, and there are certainly responses where indecent images are suggested, this word cloud shows a population engaged with the technology where upset comes from inter-actions, rather than from specific forms of content.

In Tables 3.6 and 3.7 we see an interesting difference in that while few of our respondents admit to saying nasty things to people online, they are likely (over a third of respondents) to have received some form of abusive comment or content.

In developing the knowledge of this engaged population we also wished to explore their "online confidence"—how knowledgeable they felt they were about online issues, and whether they could protect

Table 3.6 Made offensive online comments

Have you ever said anything nasty to someone on line?	*(%)*
Yes	14.4
No	85.6

Note: n = 4980

Table 3.7 Received offensive online comments

Have you ever received nasty comments/content online?	*(%)*
Yes	34.7
No	65.3

Note: n = 4992

themselves, asking them to strongly agree, agree, have no opinion, disagree, or strongly disagree with a number of statements (see Table 3.8).

It is interesting to see that, even with a broad age range, the majority of respondents believe they know more about the Internet than their parents do, and a significant number believe that they have a right to privacy regarding their use of the Internet from their

Table 3.8 Confidence and attitudes toward online protection

	Strongly agree (%)	*Agree (%)*	*No opinion (%)*	*Disagree (%)*	*Strongly disagree (%)*
I know more about the Internet than my parents ($n = 4990$)	24.11	26.11	20.70	19.34	9.74
It is none of my parents' business what I do on line ($n = 4929$)	9.07	12.09	22.36	29.32	27.17
I can protect the things I have put online from people I don't want to share them with	34.53	28.69	23.21	6.60	6.97

Note: n = 4877

Table 3.9 House rules

If yes, what sort of rules are there (please tick all that apply)?	(%)
Parents control access to sites I can visit	43.1
Age restrictions on Internet access	36.2
Parents can see what I look at online	50.0
Only allowed online for a certain amount of time	46.3
Not allowed online after a certain time in the evening	44.6
Only allowed to go online in family rooms, e.g. living room/kitchen	16.2

Note: n = 3282

parents. It is also very clearly illustrated that the vast majority believe they can keep their content "safe." What the responses all show collectively is a population who are confident with their Internet use, and also the signs of a generational gap between adults and young people.

We asked questions related to online "restrictions" at home—to explore how parents are engaging with their children in order to provide some level of protection. When asked whether there were any rules at home, 66.2 % of respondents said there were, with Table 3.9 detailing the sorts of rules that were being applied.

We can see a number of strategies employed by parents and carers at home around online "protection," although it is interesting to note that there is little consistency of response—while we might expect filtering or content control to be high, given that the strategy for "encouraging" home filtering has now existed for three years, we see that parental "inspection" to be far more likely than content control. Time based restrictions are also more popular than access control.

Finally, we asked who they might turn to in the event of being upset by something that has happened online. The overall response shows very much a peer and family oriented perspective on this (Table 3.10).

While looking at the population as a whole, and the volume of respondents in Key Stage 2 (years 7–9 in UK secondary schools), the level of parental involvement is not much of a surprise. However, the involvement of parties outside of the family or peer group is concerning, especially given the potentially serious nature of some online abuse (discussed in far more detail in Chap. 5).

Table 3.10 Who would you turn to for help?

Who would you turn to if you were upset by something that happened online (please tick all that apply)?	(%)
Friends	53.7
Parents	83.5
Other family member	43.0
School/teacher	33.0
Police	22.1

Note: n = 4818

In drawing together the analysis of the survey data, we have a number of interesting findings that start to challenge this concept of the passive user:

1. Young people readily engage with technology, and will usually have a number of different ways to access online services. As they get older the time they spend online increases.
2. They use online technologies for a number of different reasons (social media, gaming, communication, school work, shopping, etc.).
3. Even from an early age, young people are creating their own content and contributing it online.
4. Young people are more likely to be upset by content involving animal abuse, or by people posting offensive and abusive comments, than imagery of a sexual nature.
5. Family and friends are the people they will turn to if they are upset by something. It is far less likely that others within the children's workforce will be asked for help. We can certainly see a gulf between young people and their education, given some of the responses above.
6. Rules and methods of control of Internet access vary and are viewed by some young people as ineffective.
7. Social media is of interest to young people of all ages.
8. There is evidence of a "right to privacy" by some, who do not believe their parents should know what they do online and will go about subverting attempts to discover this.

LET'S TALK

I recently carried out a couple of assemblies (about 200 children in each) in a primary school for Safer Internet Day 2016. My assemblies tend to be quite interactive and what was very apparent very quickly was that, even at Key Stage 1, young people had a lot to talk about when it came to technology and relished the chance to do so. In this particular instance the clearest "gulf" between the young people's participation with online technology, and the knowledge of the teachers, was illustrated by the presentation of two images. Firstly a screen grab from Minecraft, the extremely popular online environment where players can build worlds, interact with each other, and people they don't know, play games, and generally roam around a completely unbound environment, resulted in a huge amount of chatter among the young people themselves, with everyone from reception age up to year 2 talking about their experiences, what they do with it, and the like. Once they were settled, we then moved on to a picture of Stampylongnose, a YouTube celebrity whose Minecraft avatar of a cat has adventures in his own Minecraft world which are recorded and posted online. A very clear gap between the knowledge of the children and that of the staff in the room arose—while all of the children (aged between four and seven) knew who Stampy was, only one member of staff did. It was interesting to note that, following discussion around Stampy, which wasn't actually about the character, more to do with the sorts of comments people post on his Youtube channel, a number of staff said they had felt that they had learned something from the assembly!

However, while this initial encounter was humorous and certainly not unusual in my experiences in primary schools, the subsequent assembly with the key stage 2 children highlighted how this gulf can present challenges when it comes to the role that the children's workforce has in protecting young people online. We explored the engagement of pupils with Youtube, in particular those who had their own channel. A small but significant minority (around 30 %) of young people in the room said they produced their own videos that they had posted online, and 10 of them said they already ran their own channel. We discussed what risks there might be in posting on Youtube and a number said that they had received offensive or abuse comments from people remarking on their videos. One boy, in particular, said he often received offensive comments about videos he posted on his channel. When asked what they did about these comments, given they were upsetting, thankfully the majority knew about reporting comments and also said they would be happy to tell their parents about what was said. However, the boy who said he regularly received abuse said he wouldn't tell his teacher because she would tell him off and say he shouldn't have a Youtube channel. Sadly, the teacher, who was in the room at the time, didn't dissuade him of this.

Again, after this assembly a number of staff said they had learned something about their pupils from this 20-minute "discussion," which on the face of it seems somewhat concerning given that they spend almost six hours a day with these children.

Perhaps of most interest to me when hearing about their learning was that we had, with the key stage 2 children, had some discussion around social media—there was a large number, unsurprisingly, of young people in the audience who already used social media (generally Snapchat and Instagram, with some Facebook use too). A couple of children asked me what I thought of children their age being on social media, but I turned it around and asked them what they thought. The general view was that as long as they were sensible, and only connected and shared with people they knew, they couldn't see the harm. And while they were aware of the risks that might manifest on such sites (abuse, approaches by strangers, offensive content), they were all clear about the reporting routes they had available to them.

I did ask them what the "legal" age was to engage with these services, and all knew that it was 13. However, no one in the room, either from the children or teaching staff, could tell me why this was. Many thought it was child protection laws, and a few said that it was because it was illegal. The fact that this age limit was driven primarily as a result of advertising law in the US (Federal Trade Commission 1998) came as a surprise to all of the staff in the room. This presented them with some challenges to the school policy around education on social media, which was "they shouldn't be on it, so we don't have to talk about it." Sadly, this microcosm of reflection upon the relationship between primary children and their teachers highlighted the fact that the education system, as it is, seems unable to provide for these young people to discuss their online lives with the adults teaching and look-ing after them in school. This is something that we will return to in this discussion and also in more detail toward the end of the book.

Young people view their relationships with technology as generally positive, and they will voluntarily engage with it. And while I myself refer to "online" lives in this discussion, one thing I often have to be reminded of is that this is one created in the minds of adults rather than young people themselves. Similarly, while we might make distinctions between the different types of technology for connectivity—for example, between fixed access devices (such as PCs) and mobiles (such as tablets and phones)—such differences are rarely recognised by young people. This technology, and the use of digital services, play such a fundamental part of their lives that they do not talk about the "online" and "offline" parts of their worlds, just what they do in their social and school lives.

However, one thing that is very apparent from a lot of my conversations, and something I have already touched upon above, is that there is little expectation that these sorts of issues will be addressed in school, let alone given the opportunity to talk about them. I can recall on one occasion meeting with a personal, social and health education lead in a school to discuss building a curriculum encompassing digital elements, where we would also include a number of year 10 pupils in the discussion. The wishes of the pupils and the expectations of the teacher seemed at odds. For example, the pupils felt that sex and relationship issues such as pornography and sexting should be address from year 7 upwards, while the teacher felt this would be "far too young" to talk to children about those sorts of things. The one comment that I felt was most pertinent in the discussion occurred when talking about putting discussion into classroom activities, particularly given that the pupils had mentioned that in a lot of cases they felt they were more aware of "digital issues" than the teachers: "We're not allowed to have opinions here are we."

This was both a challenging and brave thing for the pupil to say, and in exploring her comment in more detail, she expressed the view that there was no opportunity for discussion with teachers because, if they disagreed with them, they would be told to be quiet. While there are obviously issues in how disagreement with a teacher is communicated in class, the fact that these pupils felt that discussion on a sensitive topic would be impossible at their school because the teacher "knows best" is an area where this is not necessarily the case.

Young people's view of the education they received around "online safety" was rarely enthusiastic. Another experience during this year's Safer Internet Day was the opportunity to talk to a number of young people in the evening, in a social setting. I asked them if they knew it was Safer Internet Day. Two of them, in year 7 at different schools, said they knew because their teacher had told them. However, when I asked what they had done and whether they enjoyed it, I received the following:

Young person:	"We were shown a video for Safer Internet Day."
Author:	"OK, what was it about?"
Young person:	"I don't really know."
Author:	"Did you talk about it afterwards?"
Young person:	"No."

This sort of comment is not unusual across all of the ages I speak to. While not always the case, the typical experience of young people is an assembly with a video, or a carefully controlled lesson, with little opportunity for interaction. The videos will generally have a preventative or accusatory message: "Don't sext" or "Don't cyber-bully." A further comment from the conversation about Safer Internet Day further reinforced this: "We were shown a video then my teacher told us all to do posters about it. I'm not sure why."

While we will return to the capacity of schools to address the complexity across this subject matter in Chap. 6, as we are focusing in this section on talking with young people about digital technology, then this is a good time to reflect on the implications of this. As highlighted in the survey data above, even younger children do not show much confidence in teachers' awareness of digital issues and, coupled with the concerns raised above around being "told off" for using online technologies, this results in an environment where pastoral support is lacking or non-existent. On many occasions I have been told that the extent of education around these topics is to be reminded that something like sexting is illegal and that if they engage in such practices they are breaking the law.

Awareness of legalities is something that often arises in discussions with young people. As mentioned above, in general they know that you have to be 13 years old to be on social media sites such as Facebook and Instagram, even though most people aren't sure what the associated legislation is. Older children in general are aware of the (il)legalities around sexting; however, this legal awareness is usually from a perspective of "You shouldn't do it because you're breaking the law" rather than any mindfulness of the fact that victims of images redistributed in a malicious manner or done so without consent do in fact receive some protection in law. However, they are also fairly clear that they feel any threat of legislation is not sufficiently influential to prevent peers from engaging in such activities. The legalities around sexting, and the stakeholder responses, is something we will return to in Chap. 5.

While the fundamental legalities may be something that is presented to them within the school setting (i.e. the online safety lesson that tells them not to do something because it is illegal), the subsequent development of awareness is usually facilitated through discussions with peers, rather than teachers or parents. While the survey data clearly shows the reliance young people place on their friends when talking about digital issues, obviously this is some cause for concern if this is their primary source of learning, given that peers will rarely be in a position to provide anything other than ill-informed advice or moral support. The need to provide practical intervention will invariably require the support of others, and without confidence in the adult population, it is unlikely this support will be reached.

A further outcome from this peer support approach which is most prevalent among young people, particularly as they move into teenage years, is that coping and resilience mechanisms they develop may be inconsistent and, in some cases, risky in nature. For example, a group of young people told me that the best way to avoid identification, and mitigate risk, in engaging with the exchange of explicit images with someone was to: "Make sure your face isn't in the pic."

While we will return to the complexity around sexting in Chap. 5, this example does demonstrate that, with a dearth of effective education around both digital technology and sex and relationships, some peer originated solutions may not mitigate the risk in the intended manner.

As a final reflection on the impact of current approaches to educating young people about online safety, one that that is becoming increasingly apparent from my conversations is that, while they are becoming proficient in the "language of online safety," the knowledge depth may not reflect familiarity with the terms. At a workshop with four schools in the west of England, where between 15 and 20 young people from years 8 and 9 attended, one of the activities they were asked to do was to write down "coping strategies"—what are the sorts of things they and their peers do to address the sort of concerns that are raised through the engagement of digital technology in their lives. I have reproduced a number of comments from the young people below:

- Don't cyber-bully;
- Block and report;
- Block abusive people;

- Protect your identity;
- Report them to CEOPs (CEOP being the Child Exploitation and Online Protection Command, part of UK policing tasked with the online protection of children);
- Make sure your accounts are private;
- Don't get addicted to games/social media.

What is clear from all of these comments is that a "prohibitive" agenda is having an impact on their awareness.

In another question and answer session at a primary school, the children were given the opportunity to ask me anything they liked around online safety. Again, the questions generally took the form of "How can we prevent ... ?" whether that be abuse, viruses or strangers approaching them online.

I feel that we should caveat these observations with the fact that, given these workshops were facilitated by adults, there may have been an element of "tell them what they want to hear" regarding the sort of coping strategies proposed. Nevertheless, all of the above shows that this language is having an impact and that strategies are being proposed which will prevent things from happening: make sure your settings are private and therefore no one unwanted could access your social media; block people who are abusive and then they can't abuse you; don't get "addicted." What was far less prevalent in the commentary around coping strategies was anything involving talking to people or engaging with pastoral care professionals who might provide a level of support of counselling. I frequently hear the term "addicted" when talking about gaming or the use of social media. When asked what they mean by "addiction" there is far less clarity—some will say spending too long on a game (without really knowing what "too long" is), or that someone "has" to go on social media every break time.

That isn't to say that I never observe more complex discourse by young people around online safety; indeed recently I had a 10-year-old ask me "What do you mean by 'safety' anyway?" This resulted in a very interesting discussion around whether you could ever be truly safe in a volatile, evolving and unpredictable environment. I have also had complex discussions around motivations for behaviours and abuse, but these discussions usually come once I have established a rapport with a group and there is a level of trust. In general, the "interface" between young people and education professionals on these issues seems disconnected by a level of suspicion, which obviously does not provide a good foundation upon which to build knowledge in this area. Young people certainly believe they have a right to education in this area. However, it seems that a lot of them are frustrated by the opportunities their schools offer, which, as we have seen, results in them developing their own knowledge and coping strategies in isolation from other stakeholders.

TALKING ABOUT PORNOGRAPHY

Finally, before moving on to explore specific online "phenomena" and the associated behaviours around them, it is worth drawing on the discussions on young people's own views on policy direction, as explored in Chap. 2.

Firstly, it should be noted that access to pornography, and its potential impact on those consuming it, is something that young people are concerned about, particularly once they reach pre-teen and teenage years. While boys will, in general, be less concerned (and by their own admission more likely to access pornography), that isn't to say they have no concerns. I have spoken with many groups of boys who have concerns that "a friend" is viewing too much, with stories of how some will be accessing such content on their phones during every break in the school day. Some boys will also talk about expectations, body image and things such as size and performance anxiety. For girls, there are other concerns, such as unrealistic expectations and demands, the differentiation between sex in a pornographic context and reality, "addiction" to pornography by some boys, and similar issues such as body image and performance anxiety. However, interestingly, they also question whether this is just an issue for the youth population—on a number of separate occasions someone raised the issue as to why we seem only concerned with young people accessing such content. I tend to agree with them on this sentiment. The assumption that, at the age of majority, these issues go away, seems extremely naïve.

However, when I have spoken about government initiatives, particularly around filtering, they rarely see any benefit to this. Their responses range from dismissal of the idea as being unachievable, to comments about how there are far more serious things the government should be worried about: "If David Cameron really cared about young people being safe online, he'd do something about cyber-bullying."

What young people often talk about is that, while pornography is a concern, they are also affected by lots of other issues that occur "online," whether this is aspects of bullying and abuse, harassment, stalking, grooming, and of course issues such as sexting. Therefore, they ask, why is the government *only* concerned with pornography?

I recall asking a group of year 9 students some time ago, when the home filtering measures were first being proposed, what their biggest concern was about their use of the Internet. One young man said that his biggest concern was his mother finding his Internet browsing history. In another conversation boys in year 9 talked about "strategies" for making sure your parents do not stumble across their "porn stash," with two of them saying the best approach is to place all of the pornography in a folder marked "Homework." While these comments were an amusing and somewhat tongue in cheek, it does highlight the fact that pornography is consumed by a large number of teenagers, particularly boys, and while they know it may be frowned up, they do not believe technical measures will prevent it from happening, given its prevalence and access through multiple channels.

In illustrating this, in one workshop about controlling access to pornography, a young person, strangely I felt at first, said he no longer accesses Facebook. Given we were discussing government policy about content filtering, I asked why he had mentioned this, and he said "My timeline has too much porn on it!" It was a simple and clear observation around the use of filtering to control access to content—when this content is delivered in so many different ways, how can it be controlled? In the same discussion they talked about friends sending indecent images and videos via mobiles, posting on social media, sharing via Bluetooth, and many other methods. Their view was very much that with such a diversity of channels what will closing a single route do to prevent this? As one young man said: "It won't stop my mate messaging me nasty videos in the middle of the night!"

Another conversation I recall was far more concerning, but was equally dismissive about government attempts to prevent access to pornography. In a conversation with a 14-year-old at a pupil referral unit about these plans, following some discussion with him and his counsellor about his own consumption of indecent material, when this began, and the prevalence of access, I raised the notion of preventing access to pornography by placing filters at home. The boy's response was: "Well, that wouldn't stop me." When I asked why, he said "I'll just get one of the local sluts to send me some photos instead."

This was a difficult conversation to have with a young person, who clearly had issues around excessive use of pornography and, according to his counsellor, a wide history of family issues related to domestic violence and absent parents. However, what it did highlight was the fact that there are many options available to young people regarding gaining access to indecent images and, if one option is cut off to them, they will undoubtedly find another.

The Porn Lesson

It was clear from these conversations that, in the minds of young people, a blocking and filtering strategy will not work. As I have said earlier, this is not to say they did not have concerns. However, their focus was not on blocking but on providing effective education that would help explore these issues in an informed and non-judgemental manner. They feel this is something that needs to be explored and understood, rather than simply trying to stop it happening (which most young people are clear will fail).

I have, on a number of occasions, spoken with young people about what an "effective" lesson on pornography would look like for them. The "porn lesson" is something of a challenge in a school environment and something I have discussed many times with teaching staff, as a result of them feeling that they should be doing "something," but that they just weren't sure what that "something" looked like or how it should be delivered. And I have a great deal of sympathy with teachers trying to address these issues, with little to no national coordination on it (aside from OFSTED framework guidance; OFSTED 2015a). One can imagine the professional risk in delivering "the porn lesson"—given the potentially inflammatory nature of the subject matter, and also the lack of understanding around it.

When discussing "the porn lesson" with young people, however, what I am struck by, particularly given that this has happened on a number of separate occasions in different schools, with different demographics, is that their interpretation has a far broader focus than one might initially imagine. Young people's views on lessons on pornography rarely place the focus on the content, and will instead draw from a number of different areas:

- Expectation;
- Body image;
- Influence of media (looking also at mainstream media);
- Anxiety (both size and performance);
- Respect;
- Consent;
- Addiction;
- Psychological harm (e.g. erectile dysfunction).

In fact, the thing that seems to be discussed the least when talking about "the porn lesson" is pornography itself! What we can see from this list is that all of these topics already should fall readily into any effective sex and relationship curriculum. Certainly if we look at the work of an organization such as Brook (http://www.brook.org.uk/), their approach to education around sex and relationships will cover all of these topics. However, as previously discussed, there is little statutory requirement for schools to deliver such education.

An issue I will return to a number of times in this text is the difference between young people's views on "online issues" and that of other stakeholders. As mentioned above, once I have established a rapport with a group and they feel that they can speak freely, it seems that in the majority of topics I discuss with young people about how technologies affect their lives, they have a far more holistic view of this than seems to be the case when talking with adults. While a conversation with an adult might be along the lines of "What might be done about sexting?" "What might be done about pornography?" "What might be done about cyber-bullying?" young people will look beyond the technological facilitation and will, instead, focus on the behaviour and outcomes. While we might like to put these issues in boxes, for the young people I speak to they all fit on a continuum of digitally facilitated, sexualised culture.

And returning to a rights based perspective on these issues, what is also clear from discussions is that young people have a view on their rights around this area. They certainly believe and expect to receive education that is informed and appropriate. They expect to have a right to access information that helps them build their own knowledge around online issues, rights and responsibilities, sexuality, and so on. And they are also clear that a filtering approach to prevention means their rights are being compromised.

In the two following chapters, we will expand the complexities of young people's relationship with technology, and the subsequent issues related to safe and risk free engagement, by looking at two specific phenomena which gain a lot of attention from a prohibition perspective, and ones I have spent a lot of time exploring with young people—gaming and sexting. In focusing on specific issues such as these, the aim is not to provide conclusive evidence of a behavioural type around a phenomenon, but to offer a further challenge to policy and education strategy that views prohibition as the best solution to online safety.

NOTE

1. www.swgfl.org.uk/. Accessed 1 May 2016.

CHAPTER 4

Gaming: Violent Content = Violent Children?

Abstract Gaming is often viewed as one of the more negative aspects of children's online lives, with the blame for its negative impact placed squarely on the violent and sexual content provided in many games. However, even though gut feeling and knee jerk reaction might make this causal link, the author shows that there is little rigorous evidence to show that this is the case. Through discourse with young people he broadens the evidence base away from a focus on simply finger pointing at "inappropriate" content toward what young people talk about as their concerns around gaming. Issues such as excessive screen time, legitimised abuse and the potential for grooming have all been discussed by young people, and such risks lie not simply in "age inappropriate" gaming but across all manner of perfectly innocuous games. When abuse could result from a game such as Minecraft rather than Call of Duty, it is clear that prevention once again will not address the concerns. However, the author also makes the point that, while we focus upon the negatives, there are also many positive aspects to young people's gaming habits, and that these should not be forgotten in the rush to keep them "safe."

Keywords Child online safety · Gaming · Peer abuse · Cyber-bullying · Grooming · Education

This chapter and the next will explore young people's online behaviours through two different technologically mediated "phenomena"—gaming

© The Author(s) 2017   63
A. Phippen, *Children's Online Behaviour and Safety,*
DOI 10.1057/978-1-137-57095-6_4

and sexually explicit self-generated images, commonly referred to in the media as "sexting." This will allow for a more in depth exploration of issues pertaining to "child online safety" when explored alongside the policy direction that seeks to ensure young people are safe online.

This chapter specifically explores issues around gaming, with a focus on online gaming. It presents an argument that, once again, the focus of concern is content—young people are exposed to inappropriate sexual and violent content at an early age and this is damaging, therefore we need to prevent this from happening. This is certainly something that has attracted the attention of academics (e.g. Caplan et al. 2009; Desai et al. 2010; Rehbein et al. 2010). However, there are scholars (e.g. Griffiths 2000; Elson and Ferguson 2013) who argue that gaming's influence on society is actually far more complex than the media depicts and there are positives, as well as negatives, to be drawn.

Drawing on considerable primary data, through focus groups and interviews with "gamers" as well as discussions with parents of gamers and teachers, this chapter will explore the broader context of gaming, and present a more complex and nuanced picture of young people who engage in violent and explicit conduct in virtual environments with, again, no fora for discussion or to ask questions, either in the education or family setting.

I will also illustrate that the policy ideas, and subsequent legislative and regulatory development, put forward by the Westminster government falls short of engaging with the complexity, and reality, of online issues, and demonstrates the need for education, both school based and public, rather than content blocking and demands on industry to "do more." I will conclude by showing that the proposed "solutions" will do little to address the issues gamers face within the "online safety" context.

TALKING TO YOUNG PEOPLE ABOUT GAMING

Gaming is clearly a very popular online activity among young people. The South West Grid for Learning (SWGfL) survey data from 2015 shows that around 80 % of young people in Key Stage 2 (years 4–6) use the Internet for gaming. While this drops off as they get older, there is still a very significant majority of gamers among the teen population. However, it is also, in my experience, one of the least understood aspects of online life by adults within the children's workforce.

The concern with this gulf is that, as a result of not understanding the world in which young people exist (and the role online technology plays in this), this is something we must return to (see Chap. 6). However, this is worth flagging within the context of gaming because there seems to be a wider than usual gulf in this particular online phenomena and because, even though video games have been widely available since the 1970s, there is still considerable concern and conjecture around the harm they might cause, based more on anecdote and gut reaction than evidence. As a teacher who attended a recent talk I delivered said about gaming: "Surely if they spend half of their time looking down a gun shooting people, it's going to affect them."

In early 2015 the media reported on a letter sent by head teachers representing the Nantwich Schools Partnership in Cheshire (BBC 2015a). The letter, sent to parents, raised concerns about children playing 18 certified video games, such as the Grand Theft Auto and Call of Duty series. The letter described the concerns the head teachers, who represented 14 primary and two secondary schools, had regarding young children playing games containing "unacceptable" levels of violence and which, they suggested, could lead to the "early sexualisation" of young people. The letter continued with a threat that the schools might consider some cases to amount to evidence of child neglect, which would result in the reporting of parents of children who play such games to the social services. The stated intention of the teacher, according to the news reports, was to "help parents to keep their children as safe as possible in this digital era . . . It is so easy for children to end up in the wrong place and parents find it helpful to have some very clear guidelines."

While the letter may have originated from good intentions, it was foreseeable that less positive outcomes might have arisen from its receipt by parents. A confrontational communication between two key stakeholders in child welfare can cause divisions and conflict. This is particularly risky when claims are made regarding the welfare of children which come from a poorly conceived evidence base, and also a concern that opinion is being presented as fact in such communications.

A BRIEF HISTORY OF VIDEO GAME VIOLENCE

Concerns over the content of video games have existed for a long time— for almost as long as video games have been available. Perhaps the first concern arose from a 1976 arcade game called "Death Race." The game had a simple, points scoring premise, as did the majority of games of that age. It differed from video game peers such as Space Invaders or

Pacman in that the points were scored as a result of driving your vehicle over "gremlins," characters on the screen that, while perhaps looking like stick men, were labelled differently to avoid the implication of human slaughter. However, the game was criticised in the media and by organisations such as the National Safety Council as being immoral and encouraging violent conduct—the implication being that if users were playing a game which encouraged the running over of "individuals" in one's vehicle, they might be inclined to do so in real life (Kocurek 2012). Historically there have been similar concerns about the influence of violence in cartoons on television and film media with, again, worries that if children and young people see violent acts in cartoon form they may in some way replicate those behaviours in real life. Such concerns still exist in the present day, particularly pandering to the agenda of certain aspects of the tabloid media (Daily Mail 2009). However, a detailed academic review of the issue (Kirsh 2006) once again highlighted that evidence does not necessarily bear out anecdote, isolated study or conjecture.

Since this early concern about video game violence, there has been criticism of a wide range of games. Perhaps one of the most notorious was the first "adult" game for a video games console—Custer's Revenge— a game where the protagonist (a naked cowboy) had to negotiate obstacles on screen to get to the ultimate goal, which was to have sex with a naked Native American tied to a post. The game was promoted as "adults only" and the packaging explicitly stated "Not for sale to minors" and attracted much criticism for its content, the legitimisation of sexual violence, and the potential impact on players (Wise 1982). Ultimately the game was withdrawn from sale, but not before becoming the subject of a number of cases of litigation between different parties. These included the games manufacturer (challenging local state legislators for "prevention of sales") and the console manufacturer (for reputational damage as a result of their logo appearing on the game's packaging) (Billboard 1982).

As gaming technology and content became increasingly sophisticated, these early cases were followed by many claims of harm being caused by video games across a number of titles. For example, the Mortal Kombat series has caused controversy and a number of lawsuits since its first release in 1992 and was even debated in the US Congress (Wired 2009) which resulted, arguably, in the establishment of a body in the USA to oversee video game ratings—the Entertainment Software Ratings Board. One of the original "first person shooter" games—a game where the player has the gaming world presented from the view of the soldier engaged in the environment—Wolfenstein 3D, was withdrawn from sale in Germany due to allusions to Nazis. Perhaps the most popular original first-person shooters, Doom, has been cited in many actions and has been "linked" to the Columbine massacre and referred to by the offenders (BBC 2001), and Manhunt was cited as a motivating factor in the murder of Stefan Pakeerah by Warren Leblanc in 2004 (BBC 2004).

If we are to return to the issue of linking a single factor post-incident to a wider sense of causation, something already discussed when relating to the influence of pornography on young people, let us consider the issue of Doom in the Columbine case. The Doom and Doom 2 video games sold approximately two million copies in total (International Business Times 2013) and, in a time of lax copy protection, one can assume a far higher number of people played the game in some form. In the case of the Columbine massacre, post-incident it was noted that the two offenders both played Doom and also listened to the music of Marilyn Manson, a musician who has sold over 50 million records worldwide. Given the volumes involved, why would it be a surprise that young people in their teens would be listening to Manson's music and also playing the Doom video game? While we can evidence that they played this particular video game (among others), we cannot evidence that, as a result of playing this game, they decided to commit a horrific violent act in a school. With further investigation we could, I am sure, have shown evidence of viewing far more innocuous content that, due to its less controversial nature, would never have been associated with committing a violent act. If Doom was such a significant influencer on the behaviour of teens, why, at the time of release and subsequent use, were there not thousands, or even millions, of previously unheard of violent acts being committed by young people, driven as a result of playing such a video game? Perhaps, given our own discomfort with the nature of certain content, we look for evidence that, under closer examination, fails to hold any concrete causation.

INFLUENCE AND RESPONSIBILITY

However, even with this rich history of issues around the influence of violent and sexual video games on the population at large (children and young people in particular), there is in fact scant evidence to support the claims. While there are clearly moral concerns regarding the accessing of violent and sexualised content by young people, a recent meta-analysis of research into the influence of video game violence (Ferguson 2015) found very little rigorous evidence to support these claims and was critical of the methodological approach of previous research that argued for such a link. This author argued that perhaps the focus on content-blaming may "distract society from more pressing concerns such as poverty and education."

Gaming presents an interesting context in which to explore the frequent stance of policy makers and some legislators of finding blame in the content, together with a focus of responsibility on the gaming companies. It does seem, in all recent policy direction, that the focus of responsibility around child protection is believed to lie with service and content providers. Therefore, if gaming companies are to produce games with adult content, it is down to them to prevent young people from playing them.

There is an interesting tension between the moral and legislative position. On the one hand, from a moral perspective, we do feel uncomfortable with the idea that children and young people play video games with "adult" content, whether that is violent or sexual in nature. However, from a legislative position this is very difficult - while ratings are a useful guide to whether gaming content is "child friendly" there is little legislatively that can be done to enforce this. I have had many conversations with parents, teachers and social workers about this. Concern arises when they discover a child playing an "age inappropriate" game, or when gaming is conceived to be, of itself, bad for children. I can recall one primary school where a teacher asked children to do a presentation of their hobby—except gaming. However, we cannot, one would hope, use moral panic and conjecture as a position to develop legislation.

Once we take a step back from the moral stance on what is "harmful" and from binary decisions about appropriate and inappropriate games based simply on their content, we see a far more complex picture, one that cannot simply be solved by isolating certain games from young people and accusing parents of child neglect if they allow these games to be played at home. Discussions with young people show that the "issues" are numerous and complex, from the abusive language used by fellow gamers in a multi-play environment, to the legitimisation of homophobic terms to ridicule a player, to inappropriate advances which might be considered as grooming, and to excessive screen time.

Is it All about Content?

I like playing Grand Theft Auto because you can rape people.

During the period explored in this book, 2010–2015, I have spent a great deal of time talking to self-selecting gamers. From the ages of 6 up to 18, I have had many conversations in the form of interviews, focus groups and classes, with those young people who are proud to call themselves gamers, even though how they define this term can sometimes be complex. For example, while some consider a gamer to be someone who plays "serious" games on a console, others are insistent that in order to be a "proper" gamer, one needs to have a custom built PC and only play through a Steam account or similar. However, even though they may differ on how we might define a gamer—all show a passion for video games and a willingness to talk about something—it seems that they rarely have a chance to do so within their school day.

In the above quote, which took place during a conversation with a small group of young gamers (eight boys, all aged either seven or eight), such a comment can cause immediate concern—it is a difficult thing to hear from a seven-year-old boy.

While an immediate reaction to this might be to blame the video game for a child having such attitudes, in this case we explored this comment with the boy in more detail. Firstly, it should be stressed that the Grand Theft Auto games do not provide the opportunity to rape people. But the content, particularly the campaigns, within the games can be both violent and sexual in nature. This is why the boxes these games are packaged in have clear instructions about the sort of content within and carry certification for age appropriateness.

In this particular case further exploration of the comment from the boy clarified he was using the word "rape" to mean conduct involving any sexual activity with characters in the game. Yet exploring the wider home environment where the game was played caused more concern—his mother had purchased the game for him which he played in his room, unsupervised, for as long as he liked. His mother never sat with him while he played the game or checked the content he was exposed to.

If we are to take games providers to task on the content they provide, and how they "ensure" young people do not play them, we have to ask what they might do that they do not do already. At a recent online safety conference that I attended, an audience member challenged a representative of the UK gaming industry on the issues of child safety. This person asked, given that Rockstar Games, the producers of the Grand Theft Auto series, had made a significant amount of money from their products, why they didn't give something back, perhaps as a Corporate Social Responsibility (CSR) initiative, by funding child online safety programmes. The response from the gaming industry representative was direct and clear: "Rockstar Games do not produce games for children."

While the initial response to such a comment might suggest that they were absolving themselves of responsibility, if we take an objective perspective they are quite correct. The gaming company has taken responsibility for the communication of the content in the game through the use of Pan European Gaming Information (PEGI) ratings and the associated descriptions, a legislative requirement of video game manufacturers in the EU. If someone chooses to disregard clear guidance (e.g. a parent purchasing the game for their child), what more can the industry do? If we are to take the policy approach around ensuring young people cannot access pornography—that it is the responsibility of the service provider to make this happen—and apply this to gaming, how can the content provider ensure their content, entirely appropriate for an adult audience, is not viewed by young people? And even if they did find some magical solution to this, will it really address the issues that arise from gaming?

In my many discussions with young people about gaming, this interesting observation arises: regardless of the age of the people in the discussion they will always say that, while they can cope with "inappropriate" content, those younger than them should not be allow to play because they might be affected. This illustration of a third person effect (Davidson 1983) highlights the fact that gamers feel others would be more influenced by violent or sexual content than they are. However, my own observations from discussions with self-selecting gamers is that, in general, they are well adjusted, intelligent individuals with a passion for technology. Few exhibit signs of desensitisation and aggressive intent even though they are, generally, engaging with games that are clearly violent and sometimes sexual in nature.

One thing that frequently arose in my discussions with gamers was the level of abuse among peers that takes place within a multi-player gaming environment. In many games, such as the Call of Duty series, there is a connected gaming experience where gamers will connect with both strangers and friends to communicate via headsets (with both headphones and a microphone). In other games, facilities such as text-based chat windows might be offered in order to interact with other players. While some of this interaction is about gaming strategy or general chat, as the action gets more gripping and winning becomes more important, the language will generally escalate and become more abusive with frequent threats of violence and other forms of abuse. For example, as one 13-year-old gamer told me: "I get racist Tourette's when I play Call of Duty."

This was viewed as highly amusing by the rest of the group I was talking to and they recounted a number of insults he had given to his friends, such as threating to "fucking cut a friend's hands off" and that he "hoped his friend's mum got AIDS." Clearly this sort of language was not viewed as acceptable outside of the gaming environment, but within it there seemed to be a competition to make the most outrageous/offensive comments. And such abuse was not limited to the gamers' own peer group—many played these games on public servers and would see nothing wrong with either giving, or receiving, such abuse from strangers.

The level of abuse can sometimes be extreme, and many gamers have told me that there is no subject that is off limits when abusing another player and that the language used is generally far more extreme than that they would be comfortable saying to someone face to face. Topics such as paedophilia, sexual violence, sexually transmitted diseases and extremism (for example comments related to fundamentalist terrorism) were all viewed as perfectly acceptable insults to a fellow gamer.

It is particularly amusing to hear from older gamers (around 16–17 years old), many of whom say they have "grown out" of playing games such as Call of Duty, Gears of War and similar. While some had said they had started to reflect on the morality of the games they were playing, the most frequently cited reason for this was there were too many "squeakers" in these games (a term I have heard from gamers in different parts of the country). Squeakers are younger children who aggressively play on public servers and scream abuse at fellow gamers in pre-pubescent voices. As one older gamer said "It gets a little tired when every time you go onto a game some ten-year-old is telling you they're going to fuck you up." And another commented: "You get squeakers saying if you use scoping they'll come around and fuck your dead nan."

One particular observation from my time talking to gamers is the disconnect in the use of homophobic language within a gaming environment. The same individuals who find homophobia within their own school environment intolerable would happily use terms such as "gay" or "fag" to mean that someone is poor at playing a game. When challenged on the use of such language they struggle to make the link between abusing someone on a game and the unacceptability of the language they are using—many have commented that the use of those terms in a game does not have the same meaning: they have been appropriated for a different purpose and it is therefore not homophobic to use such within a gaming environment. Which does suggest a lack of empathy within the gaming environment, where aiming to cause offence becomes the norm.

In terms of reflecting on whether it is the content of the games that encourages this level of abuse, it is interesting to note that two games/gaming environments where I heard more about abuse than any other were two we might consider to be "safer," given they don't have violent or sexual content—these being Minecraft and the FIFA game series.

On face value, it seems strange when looking at Minecraft, a collaborative, "world building" game where players build structures and interact with others within them, that it could be the foundation for abuse among peers; yet this is certainly the case when talking with many gamers. The collaborative nature of the game provides the environment to deliver abuse. Firstly, the text "chat" interface through either public servers (and therefore potentially talking with strangers) or through collaborative servers set up by a group of friends provides the means to "troll" either strangers or friends, and I have been given many examples of this. Generally younger children (aged nine and below) will talk of these issues when using public servers—most are recipients, rather than generators of abuse. The responses of children of this age seems variable—some will laugh it off, some will be shocked, some will be upset and others will be active participants in the abuse. As children get older they are more likely to admit they are the people giving abuse to others, again in the form of "banter," but in general this will be swearing, threats or comments about the capabilities of fellow players.

Another approach to "trolling" on Minecraft is to cause damage to a friend's property, buildings and designs in the game. Many "crafters" spend a lot of time creating villages, building complex structures, machinery and landscaping in their worlds. And many of their peers will take pleasure in what I often heard as "good trolling"—such as destroying a village, blowing it up, filling it with lava and all manner of other "mischievous" destruction. Such abuse might also be captured online as many gamers also use Skype or other Voice over IP (VoIP) applications to interact while building or gaming together. Therefore they can capture the reaction of a "victim" when they discover their demolished village or wrecked landscape and the recorded reaction may then end up on a platform such as YouTube for others to see. Again, a disconnect between "real world" vandalism and that online exists for a lot of players. In a conversation with a primary aged crafter he told me at great length how he had gained an invite into his friend's world where he then systematically set about destroying the buildings his friend had created. When I asked whether he thought his friend might be upset by this, he couldn't see why, and suggested that he should back up his world before he allows other people to interact with it. However, when I asked if his friend had done a similar thing to, for example, an art project he had done at school, such as physically destroying a model he had built, the crafter said he thought that would be very mean and not the same sort of thing at all. Again, as with the level of abuse perpetrated online compared to what is acceptable face to face, the online environment seems to provide a disconnect in empathy—when one cannot see the impact of one's words or actions on a peer, it is less impactful than if it were to happen in person.

While we might consider a lot of this to be "friendly banter" or similar in nature to trashing someone's sandcastle at the beach there are a couple of more worrying behaviours that arise from my discussions with gamers. Firstly, there have been instances of these sorts of techniques being used to bully with a clear intention to cause upset. Gamers will try to befriend fellow gamers to get invited onto their servers with the sole intention of causing destruction and abusing others there. There is also the issue of interaction with strangers and, particularly younger, children being exposed to the sort of violent and aggressive language and threatening abuse that they would be unlikely to be exposed to in their offline lives. This is perhaps a particular concern with a game such as Minecraft which parents often view as a "safe" game due to the benign content.

In a game such as those in the FIFA series—essentially playing soccer either against a computer controlled team or, more likely, other people, whether friends or strangers—again we might observe that the content is not something that should cause concern. After all, this is simply playing soccer. However, the FIFA games will generally be referred to as the ones causing the most anger, aggression and, in some cases, physical threats and violence. A popular term for this is "rage quitting"—being so frustrated with a defeat that the player will become extremely abusive on a headset and throw about their controller (I spoke to a gamer who had broken four Xbox controllers while playing one of the FIFA games) or even their console. While rage quitting seems to occur as a result of playing many games, FIFA seems to be the one that causes this the most. A lot of gamers find those who do "rage quit" very amusing and will record their reactions, often sharing them on YouTube for others to see and potentially mock.

In exploring how gamers deal with abuse—given that many say they find excessive, aggressive abuse annoying or upsetting—it is interesting to note the "closed" nature of this. The usual approach to this is to "block" the abuser rather than report XBox them. If someone is being vocally abusive via a headset, some might mute them. I have also spoken to some who define their own ground rules within their own worlds and servers and will enforce those rules (such as blocking for using bad language) within their peer group. This is not something that escalates beyond the peer group to, for example, a trusted adult or teacher. Even in the case of the abuse coming from a stranger, it is very unlikely they will raise this issue outside of their gaming group. For the majority, the fear is that if they do tell an adult they might not be able to play the game anymore.

However, as mentioned above, perhaps the most significant observation I would make from talking to gamers about peer abuse is a normalisation of aggressive abuse, violent threats or virtual destruction, and many gamers struggle to appreciate why such behaviour could be viewed as negative. It demonstrates a lack of empathy between peers regarding the upset their actions might cause. Even when talking with two 13–year-olds about a physical fight they had as a result of one of them damaging the others Minecraft world, they struggled to recognise the extreme nature of the behaviour or the response. We also discussed the case in Plymouth of a man attacking a 13 year-old-boy after an argument in a multi-player came of Call of Duty Black Ops (Daily Mail 2009). While concerns were shown, many of the gamers weren't too surprised this sort of thing had happened because anger can spill over into the real world.

FURTHER ISSUES ARISING

In further considering issues around gaming, one thing that often arose was that of screen time. Many gamers spoke about how long they will play for, particularly if unchallenged. It was not unusual to hear of gamers who had "pulled all-nighters" in order to gain high prestige levels, or simply became immersed in the environment and lost track of time. In general there was little concern about this—while a number said they had come to school tired after a long gaming session they felt that, long term, there was little impact.

This, again, conflicts with the concerns of adults, such as teachers and parents, who frequently spoke of concerns around how long gamers spent online and the impact of this. In particular many parents expressed concern about tired or aggressive children (as a result of tiredness or withdrawal from the game) and there have certainly been many studies (e.g. Page et al. 2010) that have raised concern around excessive screen time. I have been asked on numerous occasions by parents, journalists and teachers "How long should a child be online for?" as if there were some universal solution to this issue and that the application of a simple rule would resolve all the issues around screen time. Sadly, as with all things online, things are rarely that simple as such a rule cannot take into account the nature of the interaction, whether this is passive consumption or active engagement, or the level of engagement (e.g. single task or multiple activities). There is rarely a one-size-fits-all "solution" to any of these sort of issues. Would we ask "How long is it appropriate for a child to play with a toy?" without considering the other factors?

One aspect of screen time that also frequently arose was observations by gamers around being allowed to game for long periods if it was convenient for their parents or carers to do so—while many spoke of being told to get off games if they were on them for too long, others said that on different occasions their parents seemed to be happy letting them play for as long as they liked if they were quiet. One 13-year-old boy raised this issue with the comment: "You know what Call of Duty (C.O.D). actually stands for don't you? Children's Online Daycare!"

He said a number of times his parents has left him alone to play on his games while they went out because they felt as long as he was gaming he wasn't getting into any trouble.

These observations are not presented to be critical of any one party in this multi-stakeholder world of online safety. They are simply presented to show that there are no easy solutions or simple prohibitive rules to govern "safety" when considering gaming. If we move away from viewing games as a passive, content focussed medium, we can explore them more as they actually are—as massively connected online environments which provide a level of interaction with peers and others with a common interest in the games provided.

Risk within gaming environments rarely arises from content consumption. It is far more likely that the risks associated with games come from interactions within the environment, such as upset experienced as a result of abuse. There is also an area of concern that seems rarely to get discussed within the context of child online safety at present, and that is the risk associated with contact with strangers and the potential for grooming.

The recent IPCC investigation related to the murder of Breck Bednar[1] highlights this point. Breck was befriended and groomed by someone four years older than him via gaming servers, where the abuser established a small group with access to "exclusive" servers for the game they were playing—Minecraft. Over a period of time the abuser, Lewis Daynes, isolated Breck from his family and ultimately paid for Breck to visit his flat, where he murdered him. While Breck's mother had contacted the police to relate her concerns about Daynes the Independent Police Complaints Commission (IPCC) inquiry highlighted failings to recognise these concerns as grooming, with the call handler even recording "Nothing to suggest this is grooming."

This case was a sad reminder about the use of gaming platforms for grooming—it is not just social media where online contact happens. In a massively connected community of online peers, *everyone* shares a common interest, and we can see how such environments would be targets for groomers—they have potentially a large pool of victims to access, and they have the "common interest" in which to befriend them before moving toward the standard practices of isolation and private communication (Whittle et al. 2013).

I have certainly come across a number of different occasions where gamers have raised the potential of grooming in the interactions they have had with strangers online. Usually the operation of the groomer takes the same form—befriending in a public server then attempting to take the target away from the public setting to a private one—generally by asking if they have a Skype, email or mobile they can be contacted on. While, in general, young people are fairly resilient to such approaches— clearly messages around "stranger danger" in schools still exist and are effective—what is perhaps concerning is that these approaches are not viewed as unusual or anything to be worried about. In every single potential case of grooming I have come across when talking to gamers about approaches from strangers the response is usually consistent— ignore the individual in the first instance and block them if they are persistent. While younger gamers have mentioned telling their parents about the approaches, at no time has anyone ever said they reported the approach to the police or raised it with their school. In a single workshop in a primary school, four 11-year-olds talked about the same approach (someone telling them they were good at the game, then asking if they had Skype so they could talk about gaming), but no one in the group thought it was anything to worry about.

But Let's Not Forget the Positives

In reflecting on the findings coming from conversations with gamers, it might seem that gaming presents the worst of the online world with abuse, risk and exhaustion a regular part of a gamer's life. But such a conclusion highlights one of the challenges when conducting research in this field. Sometimes we can get bogged down with the negatives, because these are the things the policy makers, media and other stakeholders want to hear about. At the time of writing, recent media attention from the Childwise survey (Childwise 2016) into young people's use of online technology, which states that children spend more time online than watching television, seemed to be desperate to find a problem with this, rather than acknowledging generational changes in the use of digital technology. Yet it seemed that even with a great deal of effort on the part of the media channels, they struggled to find someone who could point out why this change in behaviour was a problem.

There are many positives to draw from my conversations with gamers, who were, on the whole, very likable, well-adjusted, intelligent young people. Clearly they had a passion for gaming, and found the opportunity to talk about it unusual and welcome. In some cases (particularly for younger children) it was often difficult to keep the conversations clear and focussed, mainly due to the keenness of the participants to talk about what games they liked, what they did with those games, or even things like telling me about their village on Minecraft, a goal they had scored against their friend on FIFA, or even things like the configuration of their console or PC.

What I see is a great deal of keenness, albeit unfocussed, for young people to turn their passion for gaming into a career. While the majority have no clear idea how to go about this, they are, as a result of their interest, developing an understanding of various aspects of technology, such as computer graphics, networking and programing that will certainly provide a foundation for future careers. Others I have met stated they wanted to work in the creative side of the industry, and some were already developing portfolios to showcase their creative talents. Even at a fairly early age (around 11 or 12) I have spoken to young people who are learning to code because they want to write, for example, their own mods (game modifications) for Minecraft to install on the servers they have set up and to share these with friends.

Other positives that arise from discussions with gamers include social interaction. While some may view being online as in some way a lesser form of social interaction than, for example, participating in team sports, this is still a participatory, collaborative environment where friends and peers meet up and play together. For some gamers, particularly in more rural, isolated locations, this meant they were experiencing far more social interaction than would have been possible in the physical sense.

Also, many gamers raised the fact that gaming is in fact something they simply enjoy doing as "chill out time"—while it might seem strange to think that sitting down engaging in violent interaction might result in relaxation, many gamers were clear this was escapism for them. It let them forget about the day at school, or the stresses in their lives, and it was viewed as a very positive thing for them.

Addressing the Gaming "Issue"

What is clear from my work around gaming is that a policy that centres around content, blocking or prevention will do little to address the wider issues in gaming. While PEGI ratings certainly play a part in informing purchasers of these games as to the sort of content they contain and the wider playing options (e.g. providing online multi-player options), they are certainly not a guarantee of prevention and, in most cases, seem to have little impact on ensuring young people do not play "age inappropriate" games. Moreover, the gaming "phenomenon" demonstrates very clearly the need to respond to an effective, broad evidence base rather than knee-jerk judgements based upon gut feeling. While there is clearly concern around video game violence, similar to pornography's influence, the research is disparate and inconclusive. Therefore, claims of "inappropriate" gaming content leading to early sexualisation can be unhelpful, particularly when presented as fact. As can be seem from the attempts to relate a game like Doom to violent gun crime, causation does not necessarily come from correlation, especially if variables are isolated from other factors or are unduly relied on without looking at the big picture.

I have visited many schools who say they have a problem "with gaming." However, when we reflect on what staff members mean by this, it is rare that gaming is the issue: it is more likely to be something related to peer abuse, where gaming was simply the vehicle for this—in the same way that problems "with social media" usually means the digital facilitation of abuse with social media as a platform for this. It is important to appreciate the wider issues involved in gaming, and not to look at it in isolation—the issues around grooming, abuse and respect are all things that, while manifesting in gaming platforms, exist far more widely than simply within this phenomenon. Every online environment presents the opportunity for abuse, particularly with the perceived emotional disconnect that comes from not seeing the impact of abuse on the recipient. By looking at these issues in isolation we can sometimes forget about the broader issues being raised, and we therefore fail to promote holistic interventions.

Note

1. www.breckfoundation.org. Accessed 1 May 2016.

CHAPTER 5

Sexting: "The Teen Epidemic"

Abstract Sexting has been a media, and child safety, obsession for as long as the term came to prominence. The author proposes that the media focus on a world where endless teens readily engage in the exchange of indecent images of peers conflicts with the reality of a far more complex but less headline grabbing environment in which young people are growing up. He argues that the complexities of sexting cannot be addressed through simply telling young people not to do it, or threatening them with laws that were placed on the statute at a time when such practices were not envisaged. He shows that young people describe sexting as an act within a more complex environment of respect, consent and esteem, and simply being told "just say no" will do little to prevent a vulnerable teenager from engaging in such an activity. Again, the need for education is paramount, with safe, supportive environments for young people to be able to discuss the issues around these practices. Also required is an understanding of the underlying root causes, as well as the connections between mental health issues and digital behaviours.

Keywords Child online safety · Sexting · Peer abuse · Consent · Esteem · Legislation · Education

This chapter will explore in detail the phenomenon of sexting, or the self-generation and distribution of sexually explicit images. It presents a different perspective as an online phenomenon compared to gaming since

© The Author(s) 2017
A. Phippen, *Children's Online Behaviour and Safety*,
DOI 10.1057/978-1-137-57095-6_5

it is primarily (although not exclusively) a mobile facilitated issue and one that has its foundation in sexual relationships. However, as with gaming, the focus of some literature and virtually all media coverage has been on the act itself—the taking and distribution of the image, the proportions of populations of teens that are doing this and the potential issues that arise. For example, the chapter title itself is drawn from a *Daily Mail* front page headline that reported upon some work (Phippen 2012b) I carried out which showed very clearly this was not an epidemic.

I first started working around the sexting culture back in 2009 with the South West Grid for Learning (SWGfL) (Phippen 2009). We conducted a survey with schools in the South West of the UK that at the time reported a figure of 40 % of 1000 14–16-year-olds saying they knew someone who engaged in the practice. At the time, such a statistic was considered far too high, even though a similar piece of work carried out by MTV/Associated Press in the USA in the same year returned a similar value (33 %).

More sophisticated research was conducted by Ringrose et al. (2012) for the National Society for the Prevention of Cruelty to Children (NSPCC), and was one of the first pieces of research that engaged in qualitative discourse with young people on this topic. These focus groups and interviews showed that sexting was used in some schools for bullying, blackmail and harassment—extending the understanding of the topic and acknowledging that the act is not simply something that takes place between couples with little repercussion. It is this perspective on sexting that will be explored in this chapter, again as a way to demonstrate the complexity of "child online safety" and how preventative strategies fail to address the issues that can arise.

Initially I will draw on some early survey work that has been reported upon in the past but not within the broader, historical reflection on our understanding of sexting and how we might better understand the issues surrounding the practice to fit it better within the context of child online safety. The first part of this is the survey work from the SWGfL.

Following this historical review, we will then focus on the act of sexting more specifically. We continue by drawing extensively from experience with young people in schools (discussions, interviews, focus groups, classroom activities). This evidence will show that sexting does not exist in isolation and is actually a facet of online courtship, interaction and, in some cases, harassment, rather than being a phenomenon in its own right. We will explore the practice of sexting as viewed by teenagers and consider how, why and when it occurs. I will make the case that, by pigeonholing the practice into a single term, we are ignoring the complexities of the practice—the need to be popular, the wish for a relationship, the need to feel attractive or desired. I will not consider the various motivations for engaging in the activity which draw on numerous issues such as external influences, technological normalisation and attitudes toward gender.

A Brief History of "Sexting"

Sexting—the self-generation and distribution of explicit images to either one or more recipients—is a modern phenomenon which is rarely out of the media (e.g. Table 2.1). The focus of the media is mainly on the act of sexting and the subsequent fallout (e.g. a teenager being bullied as a result of an image being distributed far wider than the intended recipient), as is illustrated by the headline at the start of this chapter. As mentioned above, given my involvement with this news report, and the underlying research, and having conducted a number of focus group activities in schools to discuss the culture that exists around sexting, the headline was something of a surprise, because the report made is clear it was NOT the case that all teens were doing this. However, the point was made that it was the case that most teens were aware of instances where this had happened in their school, or within their peer group.

Looking back on key aspects of sexting also shows how reaction and attempted policy direction have focussed on the technology, although, arguably, this is one area of "teen behaviour" which policy makers have struggled to come to terms with, given the confusing legislative responses and attempts to apply dated legislation to emergent behaviours. Note that the "teen behaviour" referred to is deliberately in quotes—as this review demonstrates, this is not a behaviour that ceases once childhood ends.

The term "sexting" was a media creation, referring to the sharing of explicit text messages and self-generated images (Multimedia Messaging Service—MMS being available in 2002) in the early 2000s. The focus of the media at this time was not on the teen population, but on the behaviour of celebrities. Possibly, the first high profile use of the term referred to the Australian cricketer Shane Warne, in 2005, in a report in the Australian *Sunday Telegraph Magazine* (Roberts 2005).

The real media interest in young people and sexting, sadly, usually results from a serious incident. One of the first of these was in the USA with the suicide of Jesse Logan (Nobullying 2015a). Jesse was a teenager who sent her boyfriend a nude image which was subsequently distributed to others in her school and she was severely bullied, which ultimately resulted in her committing suicide. In 2012 Amanda Todd committed suicide (Nobullying 2015b) after three years of abuse as a result of a sexting related incident she had carried out when she was younger with a stranger on a webcam. Both of these cases received significant media coverage and elicited a great deal of debate around such behaviour.

Certainly up to this point the main focus on sexting "prevention" had been around legislation—with both US and European cases of teens who had become victims of the further distribution of images of themselves being threatened with prosecution under the relevant legislation related to the making and distribution of indecent images of children (Tang 2013; Stone 2011; Srinivas et al. 2011), something we will return to later in the chapter.

Sharing Personal Images and Videos among Young People

The above heading is drawn from the 2009 report by SWGfL (Phippen 2009) which conducted some earlier exploratory research into the sexting "phenomenon." At the time it was conducted it was considered too risky to say the research was into "sexting," hence the title it was given. When the survey instrument used to collect the data was being put together, and run past a number of validation checks, such as working with school teachers and also advisors with the children's charity Barnados, it was pointed out that such work would have to be conducted in a highly sensitive manner because the terms, and behaviours, were considered highly risky and had the potential to cause both offence and upset for those being asked to undertake it. While such concerns seemed to be expressed by most people we had spoken to about conducting the research, the motivation for doing it was that the majority of secondary schools with whom we were working at the time had expressed concerns around "sexting incidents" in their schools.

It is interesting to note how, on the one hand, we seem to have moved forward a great deal from this point, but also how, on the other hand, we still see such concerns today. It is rare I encounter a school where they do not have to deal with sexting incidents. However, there is little national guidance on this, something we will explore in more detail below. However, at the time I still encountered resistance in some schools to engaging in discussion around this topic because "it might encourage pupils to do it"—a view that was very much the case back in 2009.

One immediate stark contrast regarding these attitudes was given by a group of young people with whom the original survey tool was reviewed prior to it being disseminated. A meeting was arranged with the "senior" (i.e. Key Stage 4) pupils from the pupil council at a secondary school in the South West of the UK. This was conducted after a review by staff and Barnados, with the previously mentioned discourse around sensitivity and potential risk. The council members were told we wanted their input on something sensitive—specifically some research into the prevalence of sexting among teens. At first council members said they weren't aware of the term, but when it was explained to them one said: "Oh yeah, that happens all the time here." This was followed by much laughter from their peers.

On further discussion it became apparent that while the pupil didn't mean that everyone in the school was engaged in such activities, there was usually a "sexting incident" being discussed by teens around the school and there were some "persistent offenders" exhibiting cyclical behaviour—they would create an image and send it to someone, the image would be distributed widely and abuse would result; when the abuse died down, they would do a similar thing again.

While this was a fascinating discussion, which did reassure us this was something that merited research, we felt that, due to the exploratory nature of the work, we would just focus on quantification, rather than in-depth exploration into motivations and behaviours.

While the results from the survey have been published elsewhere, it is worthwhile drawing on a couple of key points here, in order to "set the scene" for future research, as well as putting some points forward that will be explored in more detail later in this chapter.

In one question, we asked what our respondents felt would be an "inappropriate" image—aiming to determine what might make some sort of a benchmark of acceptability among our respondents. The responses were very interesting, as they reflected a far more liberal attitude than we might have expected (see Table 5.1).

While we failed to ask whether there would be a gender difference in the "topless" image option, we still had 12 % of respondents saying they saw nothing wrong with a naked image (and 33 % saying a topless image isn't inappropriate). In expanding the opportunity for respondents to

Table 5.1   What is inappropriate?

What do you think an "inappropriate" image might be (please tick all that apply)?	(%)
Young people playing in a public place	13.3
A young person or people in swimwear at a beach	20.7
A picture/video of someone in their underwear	55.7
A picture/video of someone topless	66.6
A picture/video of someone naked	87.9
Something else	14.7

Note: n = 1121

elaborate on what they considered to be inappropriate, we received some very interesting open text responses:

- Margaret Thatcher naked on a cold day;
- Erotic man porn;
- Some people naked together in a bed;
- People having sex;
- A picture of my nan;
- I think they are all fine (in the right context);
- Men beating their meat in public;
- People throwing poo at each other and urinating on each other;
- A picture of a large hairy man wearing a revealing bikini;
- Wanking;
- A naked guy in a banana suit, some sheep in a bath tub, someone eating themselves, chicks with dick.com, two girls one cup, meat spin, lemon party;
- Nothing is inappropriate. I like to fuck. Big deal. You can all go fuck yourselves for this.

From these responses from 14 to 16-year-olds, which range from the humorous to the aggressive, we can see a broad awareness of sexual discourse, and also some level of imagination in what constitutes inappropriate. However, we can also see that it seems that sexual references are the point for some when an image becomes inappropriate.

In addressing the question around teens actually engaged in sexting practice we did not directly ask "Do you do this?" because we did not expect such a direct question to be successful. And we were more

Table 5.2 Awareness of sexting among peers

Have any of your friends shared intimate pictures/videos (perhaps with few or no clothes on and intended to be private) with a boyfriend or girlfriend (sometimes referred to as "sexting")?	*(%)_*
Yes	37.6
No	62.4

Note: n = 1139

Table 5.3 Further distribution of images

Are you aware of any times where such a picture/video was shared further than just the person it was sent to (to a third/fourth or even more people)?	*(%)*
Yes	55.9
No	44.1

Note: n = 1128

interested in awareness of "sexting culture" than to quantify how many teens are actually engaged in it—even though the media and policy makers, in my experience, are constantly after such a figure (see Table 5.2).

As mentioned above, this figure was viewed by many at the time as far too high. However, when I have quoted that figure to young people in workshops in more recent years, they usually say that they find the figure to be low.

Exploring whether such images are communicated beyond the intended recipient is important as this is the fundamental issue with sexting - the redistribution is usually what causes the upset, rather than the taking and sending of the original image. In exploring this, the statistics below revealed an interesting juxtaposition. While the majority of respondents said they were aware of images being sent beyond the intended recipient, a far smaller proportion believed this was done to cause upset. Which does pose the question: why would they be sent further if not to cause upset? (see Tables 5.3 and 5.4.)

A further interesting statistic, particularly when considering the focus of abuse as a result of further distribution of the image, is the view as to where the responsibility for the image lies. Only a very small percentage of

Table 5.4   Intention to cause upset

Were the images/videos used in a way intended to upset someone?	(%)
Yes	21.9
No	78.1

Note: n = 1114

Table 5.5   Responsibility for the image

Whose responsibility is the image/video?	(%)
The person who took it	65.5
The person in it	27.6
The person who received it	6.8

Note: n = 1129

respondents viewed the responsibility as lying with the recipient of the image—most believed either the person taking the image, or the person in the image (usually the same person in a sexting incident), was responsible for the image (Table 5.5).

LET'S TALK ABOUT SEXTING

The survey discussed above provided a snapshot of attitudes toward sexting back in 2009. While it was nowhere near a perfect data collection tool, it did produce results that provided much food for thought to explore the "sexting phenomenon." In particular it started an exploration of the wider issue of what it is like to grow up in a digital world, rather than simply aiming to quantify the act of sexting.

As such, it has resulted in something that has been a regular topic I find myself returning to again and again in my work with young people and the associated children's workforce. There are a number of reasons for this. Sometimes, it can be a specific focus, for example work with the NSPCC, discussed below, which aimed to explore the culture of sexting with young people, and sometimes as a response to a request by a school who wish to address the issue in, for example, an assembly or a workshop. However, it is equally likely that the topic will arise when talking to young people more broadly about how digital technology affects their lives, particularly those in the Key Stage 4 (and increasingly Key Stage 3) age range. The issue arises as it is clearly something that has an impact on their lives, and the lives of their peers. This is something that was brought to the fore very early in this book by the quote from the young person in Chap. 1: not all young people engage in "risky" and "dangerous" practices. Nevertheless, they are aware of these things going on, and they will certainly be on the agenda for discussion during the school day and beyond. However, we, as an adult population, will tend to respond to the extreme, rather than the normal, when we hear about these situations. As said by a 14-year-old boy I was speaking to a number of years ago:

> You know, 95 % of sexting you never get to hear about because it is an image exchanged between two parties in a relationship, and when the relationship breaks down, the images go too. You only hear about sexting when it goes wrong.

Maturity on these issues is something I often hear from young people. They have developed pragmatism around these issues (possibly, as explored below, as a result of the mundanity of recurrence of these practices) and also an understanding that they happen against a wider backdrop of growing up in the digital age.

The remainder of this chapter will explore these conversations against the wider discourse of policy thinking and attempted legislative response. Throughout 2015, there were a number of high profile media stories that raised issues around the complexities of sexting, and the failure of those tasked with the care of young people, to address them in a constructive, measured manner. In this discussion, a point I aim to make, and continue to return to, is that we cannot look at these things in isolation.

I am often asked by journalists: "Why do you think teenagers sext?" And my usual, somewhat facetious, response is: "Why wouldn't they?" I find the question strange—why wouldn't teens conduct practices that are clearly engaged in among the adult population, as the media is keen to remind us whenever a celebrity gets "caught out" doing a similar thing? Do these messages from the media and wider society demonstrate that this is "usual" behaviour within relationships? And given our obsession with the importance of celebrity, and the need to have relationships among celebrity, why would young people not explore such acts? The main difference between now and previous generations is the availability of digital technology to capture images and distribute them very quickly, to an intended recipient, but also far wider than that. The speed and potential audience are the things that are different for this generation, as the behaviours have existed far longer. This is illustrated by the decline in sales of Polaroid cameras which, in the 1970s and 1980s, provided the opportunity for owners to take "private" images without the potential embarrassment (and risk of breaching decency laws) of taking the images to be developed.

What was missing from the behaviours of couples in the past, however, aside from the potential embarrassment of someone stumbling across a collection of photographs, or being passed around among peers, was the easy means to reproduce and distribute such a photograph. Reproduction was costly and time consuming. However, now it is easy and instant and it is this that raises the risk when engaging in this practice. Although, to return to the above quote, it might be better to reclassify the risk of sexting not in the taking and sending of a personal image to an intended recipient, but the unauthorised distribution of the image to further recipients.

Popular Girls Don't Sext

Again, this exploration is intended to illustrate the complexities of the connected world in which young people grow up in and how preventative measures are rarely the solution. It also highlights the maturity of young people reflecting on these digital behaviours that we, the adult population, seem to struggle with. On a number of occasions when exploring sexting culture with teens, I have had, generally, girls saying that it is in some way flattering to receive a request from a popular boy for an image. However, when others in the group, with a more cynical and, arguably, realistic, perspective on the practice have intervened and highlighted that a "lad" will rarely just ask one person for an image, the flattery does somewhat lose its shine.

The quote about popular girls not sexting was from a 14-year-old boy in a session discussing sexting "culture." It was a boys only group, so there was much laughter and "banter" among them at the start of the session which was, they said, the first time they'd had a chance to talk about these things with "a grown up." However, once the giggling had died down and they had stopped discussing incidents they were aware of, the gist of the discussion was that yes, there were incidents around their peer groups and that there were generally one or two incidents ongoing at any given time.

When talking about the sort of people who do engage in such practices, there was some talk about peers they knew who were either always pestering a girl for an image, or volunteering an image to a girl as a means to "ask them out" or to look to form a relationship with them. And when asked what sort of girls would be most likely to respond to such a request, the above quote was spoken by one of the group.

He elaborated on this point with some incredulity—of course, he said, popular girls don't need to do this sort of thing, they already have partners and therefore do not need to respond to requests for images in the hope that someone will embark on a relationship with them. This is a fundamental issue around a lot of my discussions with young people about technology and relationships—behaviours merely underpin a desire to be attractive, to be popular and to have a relationship with someone. The need for popularity, the need to have your own attractiveness reinforced by being in a relationship, seems to start at an increasingly early age. In a recent discussion group with year 6 pupils, where the discussion topic was supposed to be whether digital technology had any impact on esteem, body image and the like, within 10 minutes of the discussion starting (a mixed group of 10 and 11-year-olds) the young people broke into a spontaneous discussion about who is "going out" with whom—with the majority of the group keen to tell me that they have either a boyfriend or a girlfriend. While at this age there is virtually no discussion around how technology facilitates sexual encounters and the like, it is clear at this age that "going out" with someone does place you higher in terms of popularity than those who are not.

Returning to the discussion around popular girls not sexting, what resonated here were conversations I had had with senior leaders in schools who had dealt with sexting incidents. On a number of occasions, I have been told the victim—generally someone who had produced and sent an image to someone who had then distributed the image further and as a result the victim had been the subject of some level of abuse—was "not the sort you would expect to do this sort of thing." When questioned about why they were not the sort of person one might expect to do this sort of thing the answer is usually something along the lines of the victim being one of the less popular pupils in the year, generally quiet, one of the less visible children in class.

One of the more surprising things, from my own perspective as a parent in his forties who has done research around the public engagement of technology for almost 20 years, I find in my discussions with young people around sexting is how mundane they view this sort of thing, which I suppose isn't surprising given the number of incidents they might be aware of in a given year. The view is usually one of acceptance and "let's get over it"—yes people do it, and yes these images often get sent far beyond the intended recipient, and sometimes the person in the photograph will receive abuse as a result; but is it really that big a deal?

In reflecting on this, I find it interesting from my own perspective that I would have once said I found this shocking—however, being engaged, if not immersed, in such a culture for a number of years now I feel I have in some way also become somewhat used to these incidents arising and the same attitudes and reactions manifesting. Perhaps the biggest concern is that the focus is on the act, rather than the abuse a victim may receive as a result.

The sense seems to be that an incident "gets old really quickly," meaning that any shame, or resultant abuse, will pass quickly. They will generally acknowledge that the level of abuse a victim receives will have less to do with the act itself, and more to do with the popularity of the individual in the first place. So someone who might be resilient and be able to "laugh off" an incident is less likely to receive a prolonged period of abuse than someone with whom the abusers can see they are getting to. However, in general most of the young people I speak to about sexting and similar practices are not empathetic with the potential impact of abuse on the victim. Even though many are familiar with cases such as Jessie Logan and Amanda Todd they seem surprised that abuse can result in suicide. It seems that these cases, both being in North America, are sufficiently removed from the localised nature of most young people's lives to make it unlikely they will relate these outcomes to their own peer groups. It is interesting, however, to observe that the vast majority of teenagers I have spoken with are aware of Amanda Todd and her abuse, they just can't empathise with it.

Returning to the nature of abuse, because, as discussed above, when we are looking at the issues that arise from sexting, it is rare that we are focusing on the act, more the fallout as a result of further distribution and others seeing the images or videos. What is interesting to note about the nature of abuse that arises from such scenarios is that it will invariably centre on the person in the image. It is probably fair to say that, in the majority of cases, but certainly not all, the victim of abuse will be female, and the abusers will come from both males and females within the peer group. The focus of abuse seems to be on the victim being a "slut" for sending such an image—this will generally be the view of female abusers with a female victim and to some extent male abusers too.

When challenged on this, young people will happily acknowledge that they will probably know others who have done such things and, in some cases, abusers will have also engaged in such practices; but the victim's "mistake" is they got "caught out." I have also often questioned why girls would turn against other girls, particularly as they acknowledge the behaviour of the victim is not unusual. Sometimes girls tell me they think that the victim will be abused because they are getting attention from boys that the abusers would like themselves. On a number of occasions, I have also had young people say they will join in with the abuse because it will detract from the potential for them to be subject to bullying. In joining in with the pack those who are less popular or have been subject to abuse themselves can divert attention from them onto another victim. Which harks back to a previous comment about how the popularity and resilience of the victim plays a large part in how quickly such abuse will subside.

What is far less likely is that the recipient of the image, and generally the person who passes the image on further and who is the catalyst for the abuse, will be challenged on their behaviour. This is an interesting point often acknowledged by young people yet rarely explained to any satisfactory level. If we return to the statistics from the 2009 survey on sexting, we could see then that our respondents overwhelming said that the responsibility for the image lies with the person taking or appearing in the image, not the recipient of it.

Reporting, or any form of disclosure around sexting, is particularly low—it is highly unlikely that a victim of redistribution of images would report this to an adult. It would have to be, I am told, a very serious issue before anything related to sexting would break out of a peer group and an adult was involved. The reasons for this are sadly recurring and not too surprising—adults wouldn't understand, they would overreact, they don't realise its not that big a deal, they would tell their parents, and so on. The most common comment, from discussion all over the country, is that they couldn't tell an adult because they "wouldn't want to be judged," which once again reflects the guilt back on to the victim of such incidents. One would hope that if a vulnerable young person was to raise such an issue with an adult, they wouldn't receive such a response—however, the expectation is that they would receive no sympathy because they should not have sent the image in the first place.

Something that is sadly a recurring theme for those who have been upset by online related incidents.

The focus on the victim's "fault" is particularly curious, given that, in a large number of cases, it will have been the recipient who has instigated the image exchange by requesting it. By far the most common practice is for a boy to ask a girl for an image, and them send it. A volunteered image by a girl was far less likely. However, for males the opposite was true—a number of discussions with boys raised the issue of particular individuals in their peer group who believed the best way to "ask out" a girl was via a mobile device, with the request underpinned with an image. The nature of this image might vary, from a topless or "six pack" shot, to something more explicit such as their genitals. Indeed, very recently I was told of an incident by a group of year 8 boys where a peer had taken an image of their genitals and sent it to two girls over the previous weekend. While this scenario has arisen many times in my discussions with young people, it is rare that anyone has a grasp on the origins of this practice, or the thought process that goes into it, particularly if the girl is not particularly well known to the boy. It seems strange that the opening discourse between two teens who may end up in a relationship is the communication of an image of the male member. The most usual "explanation" for this seems to be simply that they believe this is how relationships are formed. In the case of the year 8 boys above, they said the view of the sender seemed to be that by sending the image to two girls he was raising the chances of one of them saying yes to a relationship with him.

> I work on refineries and many men cheat on there and due to me being the only under 40 female on site for 800 guys many flirted with me sending pics of cocks.

This quote comes, not from a teenager, but a 20-year-old female I interviewed as part of a piece of work around digital behaviours in the workplace (Phippen and Ashby 2015). I often use this quote in talks I am giving on this topic to raise the difference between online and offline harassment. What I find incredible about this statement is that the individual is regularly receiving indecent photographs of colleague's genitals, but brushes off the behaviour as "flirting." It would be a highly unusual office environment where an individual declared that her colleagues were flirting with her by physically exposing themselves to her. However, given the digital buffer between exposer and recipient, as facilitated via a mobile phone, the victim is viewing the situation as a far less serious incident.

This differentiation between what is acceptable online and offline arises a great deal in my discussions with young people. For example, I have, on a number of occasions, heard girls say that they had fallen out with someone in their class. When asked why, they say that it's because they were asked to send them a nude photograph, and that they had refused. Sometimes they might be asked once, sometimes they might be asked a number of times. What is a particular concern is that this is viewed as normal behaviour—part of class banter. I have often asked whether anyone who has been subjected to such requests had reported it to an adult; and no one has ever said they would—it was just to be expected. However, in presenting them with an offline scenario—usually the hypothetical I give them is whether it is acceptable for me to ask an administrator in my office for a naked picture of themselves during a face to face conversation —I am always told that this is unacceptable. So once again we have a legitimisation of antisocial behaviour because it is facilitated by a piece of technology—the "buffer" that softens the unacceptability of something.

A recent case that gained significant media coverage also raised the wider issues around legitimized sexual harassment and abuse. In this case (Daily Mail 2014) a drunken student was filmed by a friend slapping a sleeping girl's face with his genitals. The video was subsequently shared among his peers. In this case the victim did recognise this for what it was— sexual assault—and the offender has received a prison term. However, in exploring this with young people in schools it is interesting to observe that a number view this as amusing banter and the accusation of assault an overreaction. It is also interesting to note that there isn't a clear gender split on this view—as many females as males expressed this opinion. In one session where this case was explored, a male student called out "Yes, but was she drunk?" as if this in some way legitimised the assault. Thankfully, others in the class challenged this view.

This is certainly not the single cultural reference point where this opinion is expressed. I also use the Steubenville case in the USA, where a 16-year-old girl passed out at a party and was subsequently stripped and sexually assaulted by males. We explored the public response to the fact that the two who carried out the assault were charged and imprisoned— where most of the focus is not on their unacceptable behaviour but on how they had made "a mistake" and that it was a shame that they were imprisoned. On three separate occasions, females have expressed the same comment: "She had it coming to her."

While this is certainly not the view of the majority of young people I have discussed this with, it is concerning that the same opinion has been expressed a number of times. In trying to understand their rationale for such a response, the view was generally that, while the behaviour of the males in the case was wrong, this is the sort of thing you should "expect" if you pass out at a party. As I was told in one session, "You shouldn't get that drunk at a party unless you have a friend to look after you, otherwise you should expect this sort of thing to happen."

This demonstrates the fact that sexting is not a distinct practice, it is part of a wider shift illustrating how technology normalises unacceptable behaviour and cultural influences legitimise what we might once have felt to be offensive. Sexting is not a secluded phenomenon, it is part of growing up in a connected age where technology allows lives to be expressed on a public stage, and supported through wider influences such as celebrity and the cult of personality and the resultant abuse that also relates to cultural influences wider than just the peer group. This therefore presents challenge for us, especially if the particular ideological focus for both legislation and education policy is on prohibition and prevention of the act itself, while failing to understand and engage with the more subtle, complex, motivational and, to a certain extent, coercive aspects.

REINFORCING THE NEED FOR COMPREHENSIVE SEX AND RELATIONSHIP EDUCATION

I have visited many schools where the policy around sexting seems to be the articulation of the legal position, stating that if they engage with such practices, they are breaking the law. This does not sound like a constructive starting point to a supportive, understanding environment where a young person might be willing to disclose abuse and harassment to adults. While the position may, by the letter of the law, be correct, The Protection of Children Act, 1978 (UK Government 1978) in the UK stipulates that sending, creating and/or possessing an indecent image of anyone under 18 is committing an offence, even if that picture is of the sender. So while it is legal for two 16-year-olds to have sex, if they were to take a naked image and send it to their partner, they would be breaking the law, and so would the partner (both for being in possession and also creating an indecent image of a child). Clearly, given the date that the law passed onto the statute books, its development and underpinning debate had never entertained a time when young people would have the capability to take and distribute such images of themselves so readily with a device owned by the vast majority of the population. Therefore, when the law is applied without pragmatism, it can be viewed as unwieldy at best and in other cases draconian. More recently in the UK the Crown Prosecution Service has released more pragmatic guidance, suggesting that it is rarely in the public interest to prosecute a minor for such an incident, unless there were malicious circumstances associated with it (Crown Prosecution Service 2015).

A number of interesting legal cases and legislature were presented in 2015. Early in the year the UK government passed the Criminal Justice and Courts Act (UK Government 2015a), introducing the new offence of "disclosing private sexual photographs and films with intent to cause distress"—addressing the growing problem of "revenge porn" among the adult population. It should be stressed that this legislative protection was addressing the issue in the adult population, not the protection of minors from such incidents. Interestingly, given the usual length of time between a law being passed and it being used effectively in prosecution, it was only five months before the first offence under the new legislation was successfully prosecuted.

Also at the start of 2015, the pragmatic advice of the Crown Prosecution Service was applied in the successful prosecution of two 15-year-old boys in Plymouth, who were found guilty of being in possession of and distributing indecent images of a minor and given referral orders after one sold 78 images of his (14-year-old) ex-girlfriend to the other. This case illustrated that, while the guidance may state it is rarely in the public interest, given the malicious intent exhibited in the sale of the images the law was effectively applied in this case. However, public reaction was, again, divided, with some comments claiming that the fault lay with the victim, as she should not have taken the images in the first place. An illustrative quote from the Facebook page of a local newspaper (Plymouth Herald 2015) illustrated this:

> She sent the pictures in the first place, why hasn't she been charged with distributing images? He wouldn't have had any to sell if she hadn't sent them. These lads have got this on their record for LIFE. When they become parents, they won't be able to help at the school or go on school trips because of this. She started it all the minute she pressed "send" on that selfie.

Sadly, such a societal perspective remains in some rulings on such matters. In a recent case of child sexual exploitation that has just seen a ruling (Peterborough Telegraph 2016), a 19-year-old groomed and coerced an under-aged girl to send him photographs of herself using Snapchat. He then used those images to coerce her further into send more explicit images, with a threat of public exposure if she did not do what was requested. In the ruling on the case, while raising the abhorrence of the acts of the abuser, the judge went on to apportion some of the blame to the victim: "We have to protect girls against themselves and teenagers have to realise that conduct of this nature has consequences."

In another case this year, which received much media comment, a 14-year-old boy at a school sent an image of himself to a girl in his year, who subsequently distributed the image further. The school spoke to both the sender and redistributor of the image, and decided, as they felt a law had been broken, that both should be reported to the police. As a result of this, both ended up with a note on a police record, meaning that any subsequent criminal record check would retrieve this. The press coverage in this case focused on the criminalisation of the children and the response of the police (Ward 2015). However, this raises concerns around whether schools know how to deal with such incidents—the decision to involve the police lay with the school, and the police responded in the manner the law sets out.

Clearly these cases illustrate the complexity of applying old legislation developed to protect young people in a modern, digital context, and how applying the "letter of the law" in an educational setting can be counter-productive and further build barriers between teens and adults. At the time of writing, the National Police Chiefs Council has proposed guidelines for police forces and educational establishments which aim to address some of these challenges, particularly focussing on the need for pragmatism and victim support.

Regardless of the legal situation, this discussion once again highlights the failings in general of the educational response to this "modern phenomenon." While many schools say they have some strategy in delivering education about sexting in the curriculum, this usually involves, I am told by young people, being shown a video or short presentation, usually with a legal focus. I have rarely heard of schools where young people are given the chance to discuss the wider issues around sexting, such as boundaries, consent, respect and esteem. Once again, we focus on the act, rather than the motivations, which fails to address the complexities of the situational context around sexting. Yet I also find that young people are very keen to have the opportunity to discuss these things with an adult who does not create a judgemental environment. And of course they have questions around legality, victim protection, acceptability and the like.

What is also interesting to note is the difference in opinion between young people and education professionals about which school year should we begin to talk about sexting. Usually, from a teacher's perspective, if they believe such issues should be discussed, it should be done in the later stages of secondary school, certainly in Key Stage 4. However, the young people I have spoken to about this (usually older teens who are at this key stage) usually state that such education should come far younger—certainly at the start of secondary and perhaps in primary. When questioned on how this would work with younger children (given the concerns teachers and many other adults would express regarding exposing younger children to the concept of sexting), the responses are usually quite mature —you don't talk about sexting, you talk about things like boundaries, respect and esteem, so that when they do approach an age when sexting becomes more prevalent, they have already developed some resilience, through knowledge and discussion, to be able to deal with the issues in a more mature way. As I was told by one 15-year-old who had just told their personal, social health and economic education head that teaching on sexting should start in year 7: "It's too late for us, you need to talk to them before its happening to them."

CHAPTER 6

How Big is the Gulf?

Abstract While adults, in particular parents, may wish to prevent online abuse, access to inappropriate content and approaches by predators the author suggests that we need to understand that, while we may go some way to protecting young people through technological intervention, education is key. When looking at the educational setting within the UK, through strong quantitative data, it is seen that schools are sometimes ill equipped to appreciate and understand the complexities that online technology bring to children's social relationships and therefore are unlikely to be able to deliver effective education in this area, even with the glare of the regulator upon them. The author argues that policy failures to ensure that effective sex and relationship education, and personal, social and health education, are delivered across all schools, without national coordination, have resulted in piecemeal and disjointed education where school staff are doing "something" because they know they need to but sometimes struggle to understand what that "something" should be.

Keywords Child online safety · Education policy · 360 Degree Safe · Monitoring · Tracking · Filtering · Consent · Education

In bringing together the discussion from the previous three chapters, we will now start to develop a key thread of the book, that the British education system, and related policy, is not equipped to address the questions, issues and concerns raised by young people experiencing a hyper-connected childhood and adolescence. One thing that comes through strongly from the evidence gathered from both quantitative and qualitative sources is that while we, the adult stakeholders in this domain, like to put things into clearly defined and delineated boundaries, this is not the experience of the young people who live in this space. While we might suggest we "need to do something about sexting," young people have a far more holistic perspective around why individuals might carry out the sexting "act" and how that exists in an environment of harassment, ill-conceived boundaries and the wish to be in a relationship.

This chapter will explore both the practice in schools and also the impact of policy changes within the school environment and beyond around the issue of online safety. It will examine whether policy change and strategy has resulted in changes in practice or has had an effective impact on young people. In evaluating the impact, I will propose that the most effective educational response comes not from concern for child welfare, but from the threat of inspection.

In exploring the experiences of education establishments, and adult stakeholders in this domain, we will firstly explore the "state of the nation," drawing heavily on data from the 360 Degree Safe tool (Phippen 2010): a self-review tool which allows an establishment to assess its online safety policy and practice, currently used by nearly 7000 schools in the UK. This is an extremely rich dataset that allows us to measure how schools position themselves against a wide variety of metrics associated with online safety. Given its long term use (first released in 2009) it also allows us to test the impact of regulatory change on schools, such as the impact of the OFSTED policy change in September 2012, so as to define more explicitly inspection around online issues.

However, given the persistent ethnographic focus of this book, I will also discuss the perspectives of teachers and other education professionals through my work in schools. This exploration is based upon specific discussion around, for example, changes in policy, inspection and curriculum developments but also more generally draws upon evidence from less formal settings such as discussion with staff following workshops with young people in schools, observations when doing assemblies, staff training and "twilight" sessions, and parents talks. We will also look at other adults in the school setting, such as senior leaders and governors, to contrast their attitudes with those of young people, and also parental engagement.

I am going to start by reflecting on a specific incident that happened a couple of years ago which allows us to take an individual perspective to illustrate how wide the gulf between adult stakeholders and young people might be, and why it might exist.

A Perspective on Child Online Safety from a Parent

> I am so grateful my girls are sensible and level headed. They don't need to be advised on how to be safe on the Internet as they aren't stupid.

This quote is taken from a parent whose children had attended an assembly I did at a school in the South West of the UK. I had been asked by the school to do two assemblies. The first was for years 7 and 8 and looked at behaviour on social media, along with some slightly more serious topics such as online harassment. The second assembly was for year 9 and 10 pupils and explored these issues in more depth and also looking at more "adult" topics such as sexting and adult content. The parent quoted above had two girls in year 7, and she was upset that her girls attended an assembly she considered to be inappropriate for children of their age. I should stress that the assembly, in my view, and also that of the school, was that it was entirely age appropriate. While subjects such as sexting and pornography were touched upon, they were not referred to explicitly, the focus being more that, in the case of pornography, young people might be exposed to content that we might view as inappropriate for children their age and which may be distributed and end up on devices even if it was not requested. And in the case of sexting, the discussion focused around people who might ask you to do things you might be uncomfortable with, and that it was all right to say no.

However, the parent was drawn towards a far more isolationist view of her children's social development and, in a detailed complaint, raised a number of issues:

- Her girls were too young to hear about the subject matter in the assembly;
- Her girls didn't use social media and children of that age that did "deserved everything they got";
- Her girls might be in some way distressed by hearing about the "morally wrong" behaviours carried out by people who did use social media;
- The school should focus on academic, not social, education;
- Her daughters did not need to hear about staying safe online because they are not stupid and that those who were should be spoken to separately.

Interestingly, while the comments made by this parent may have been at the extreme end of perspectives on child online safety—that it's not their children's problem, therefore don't talk to them about it—the concerns and beliefs expressed are not unusual in my conversations with adults and illustrate one of the commonly held beliefs by adults, namely that online abuse only happens to those who engage with the online world, and therefore if they keep away they will be fine.

In developing this perspective from the view of the parent above, an issue I immediately take with this is that it assumes that "online" is something that can be contained yet fails to appreciate the diversity of digital communication and also how we build resilience from an early age rather than dealing with issues in a reactive way. Even a child with no devices will be exposed to the online world through interactions with their peers—to suggest that a child who is not using social media will never be affected by it is naïve in the extreme. Not only will they hear about the interactions of their peers on social media, they may also observe the arguments that have started online and spill over into the classroom, and they may be shown content and comment via their peers' devices, and so on.

While the quote may have been at the extreme end of parental perspectives on online safety, I have been asked many times from parents about prevention—how can they ensure their children are free from inappropriate content, cyber-bullying, predators, and so on? They often ask which piece of technology they can install to ensure none of these things happen; and my response is usually something along the lines of "you can't." While this might seem like something of a blunt approach to presenting a solution, I try to refocus away from prevention and onto resilience, education and communication. One of the most powerful things parents can do is to make it clear to their children that there are bad things online, and while they will do all they can to protect them from these things, if they do receive abusive messages and unwanted requests, or see inappropriate content, they should tell them because, unless they know something is happening, they can't do anything to help.

Returning to the quote, my response to the teacher who passed on this "complaint" was twofold. Firstly, how does this parent know her children don't use social media? I have spoken with many young people who say they have signed up to services and platforms and do not tell their parents because they know they will be told off or challenged or have the account removed. Secondly, perhaps more importantly, regardless of what the girls get up to, how can the parent prevent her children from receiving an unsolicited message, being shown certain content or receiving, via different means, some form of abuse. If the child had never received any education on the topic, or even some acknowledgement that sometimes nasty things can happen, how will he or she know what to do when it occurs? Surely a better approach is to say "All right, I know you won't do this, but someone will, so you need to be aware that this sort of thing goes on and I want you to tell me if something happens to you."

To reiterate a point made in different sections of the book, this is not the world in which young people exist and interact with, and taking a prohibitive strategy fails to acknowledge what growing up in a connected society is at its essence. The relationships, interactions and worlds experienced by young people, facilitated a great deal through online environments and tools is, to quote an excellent text on this topic, "complicated" (Boyd 2014). And complicated is rarely addressed effectively through prohibition. If we are to provide effective strategies for "child online safety," the most important stakeholder in this space—the child—needs to be engaged and supported, not "protected" and isolated. It is only the knowledge of risk, problems and concerns that allows those engaged in these environments to make judgements and to develop resilience to be able to respond effectively and safely when things do go badly.

In developing this need for underlying knowledge by other stakeholders in this space in order to be able to protect and educate young people better on online risk and their impacts, it is worth reflecting on the establishments where most education takes place—schools —and how national regulation has impacted upon their engagement in this area. If we are to assume that, in order to achieve consistent education around online safety, schools are ideally placed to do this, we need to understand whether schools are capable of delivering it.

THE STATE OF THE NATION: SCHOOLS' PERFORMANCE AROUND ONLINE SAFETY POLICY AND PRACTICE

In analysing the performances of schools around online safety, the most powerful data source to draw from is the 360 Degree Safe tool. The tool was developed by the South West Grid for Learning (SWGfL), drawing upon the experience of leading practitioners in the field, each of whom had considerable experience in the field of online safety, whether as school leaders, teachers, academics or technology experts. The tool was originally launched as an article based system in November 2009, after first being piloted in the South West region. It was then refined and launched as a web based tool. Since its launch, it has won a number of national awards and is widely recognised, including by the school inspectorate OFSTED. It is designed so that it can be used in any type of school, at a pace suited to a school's particular situation. Despite its regional origins, funding and administration, the project now involves schools nationally. And while adoption of the tool is voluntary, as is illustrated below, its adoption continues to grow, particularly as a result of the growing interest around online safety within the schools' inspectorate for England—OFSTED.

As part of the scrutiny on schools practice and governance, OFSTED plays a major part in making public judgements which are published on their website—in that way, they are an extremely powerful influencer of senior leaders in schools as a poor OFSTED inspection can result in the replacing of the management in a school.

Arguably, since the Academies Act 2010 (UK Government 2010), OFSTED now provides the only public challenge to any school that has chosen to decouple itself from local authority control. Prior to the Academies Act, the majority of schools in England were funded via local authorities—the Government gave funding to local authorities who distributed it to schools in their region and therefore had some level of scrutiny. However, since this act a growing number of schools have left authority influence and receive their funding directly from central government. Without local authority intervention, these schools have fewer layers of governance, which are reduced to the school senior leaders and the board of governors. Outside this, accountability of governance and practice is only conducted through OFSTED inspection.

Therefore, having the inspectorate define explicitly that they will be exploring issues around online safety can have a significant influence on practice in schools.

In September 2012 OFSTED released their new Framework for Safeguarding (OFSTED 2012) which was the first time the inspectorate had referred to online safety issues in their documentation:

Safeguarding is not just about protecting children from deliberate harm. It includes issues for schools such as:

    ...

- bullying, including cyber-bullying (by text message, on social networking sites, and so on)

    ...

- internet or e-safety

Paragraph 21:

Inspectors should include e-safety in their discussions with pupils (covering topics such as safe use of the internet and social networking sites, cyber-bullying, including by text message and so on), and what measures the school takes to promote safe use and combat unsafe use, both proactively (by preparing pupils to engage in e-systems) and reactively (by helping them to deal with a situation when something goes wrong).

OFSTED further defined online safety issues in their Common Inspection Framework in 2015 (OFSTED 2015b):

10. Safeguarding action may be needed to protect children and learners from:

    ...

- bullying, including online bullying and prejudice-based bullying

    ....

- the impact of new technologies on sexual behaviour, for example sexting

11. Safeguarding is not just about protecting children, learners and vulnerable adults from deliberate harm, neglect and failure to act. It relates to broader aspects of care and education, including:

    ...

- online safety and associated issues

    ....

Inspectors should include online safety in their discussions with pupils and learners (covering topics such as online bullying and safe use of the internet and social media). Inspectors should investigate what the school or further education and skills provider does to educate pupils in online safety and how the provider or school deals with issues when they arise.

It is also interesting to note in this document that "the term 'online safety' reflects a widening range of issues associated with technology and a user's access to content, contact with others and behavioural issues."

Compared to the definition of online safety from the Online Safety Bill discussed in Chap. 2, this definition is far more encompassing and acknowledges behaviours and contact as well as content. Due to the nature of the data collected by the 360 Degree Safe tool, we can explore the impact of these changes in the inspection process, which will be discussed below.

CONTENT AND STRUCTURES OF THE 360 DEGREE SAFE TOOL

Schools carry out e-safety self-reviews via a web interface, and the data are sent to a centralised relational database, which holds the information in three related tables, categorised as establishments, aspects and rating. The school gradually builds up a profile in each of the three tables by covering specific aspects of the self-review question array in turn. For each "aspect" within the tool, schools use a five-level grading system to self-evaluate their progress. We can consider that a level of 3 or above on any particular aspect signifies that a reasonable level of safety has been achieved in the school, with level 5 denoting nothing in place and level 4 proposing a developmental phase (Table 6.1).

Schools assess each item against these criteria, and they then enter their achieved level, which is then stored in the central database. Reviewers in schools are not left to their own devices when deciding upon the levels they would consider appropriate for each aspect. For every aspect in the

Table 6.1   360 Degree Safe levels

Level 5	There is little or nothing in place
Level 4	Policy and practice is being developed
Level 3	Basic e-safety policy and practice is in place
Level 2	Policy and practice is coherent and embedded
Level 1	Policy and practice is aspirational and innovative

tool, there is clear guidance and definition for each level. Alongside each level descriptor, the tool also provides guidance on how to "progress" to the next level of each aspect. This allows the school to review and develop its own performance. Schools are able to login and upgrade their scores when they feel they have reached a new level, so the database holds a record of their progress, as well as their baseline. The reviewer retains previous submissions and will allow the school to define a development plan to move their online safety policy and practice on, and which is intended to be used as (and frequently is used as) a school improvement plan. By way of illustration of the level of a specific aspect, the levels for the "staff training" aspect are defined in Table 6.2 (copied and reformatted from the core specification).[1]

In total, there are 28 aspects defined in the tool, grouped by elements (overarching themes in school governance), strands (logical groupings of aspects within elements, e.g. policies), and the individual aspects themselves (Table 6.3).

As can be seen in Table 6.3, the tool defines a broad set of metrics around which to define online safety policy and practice in schools. It is particularly interesting to note, against the policy focus discussed in Chap. 2, that connectivity and filtering is defined as a single aspect, rather than being to focus on the whole tool.

VALIDITY OF SCHOOL SELF-REVIEW DATA

The question needs to be raised as to whether schools can be relied upon to self-report their compliance situation accurately. For the purposes of this exploration, we argue that overall they can. School self-review is now considered a mainstream activity in many countries, particularly in the UK (Shewbridge et al. 2014) and New Zealand (Nusche et al. 2012), where the Organisation for Economic Co-operation and Development has recently sponsored evaluation activities demonstrating success. For some time, however, school self-review processes were seen as being potentially prone to bias and inconsistency. In its early days, Pring (1996) and Elliott (1996) argued against relying on school self-review data as a vehicle for school improvement. However, in MacBeath (1999), Mortimore and Sammons (1997), Mortimore and Whitty (1997) and Stoll (1992) we find counter-arguments disputing any lack of reliability and validity. School self-review was thought by these authors to allow a unique insight into many aspects of education and school life

Table 6.2   Example 360 Degree Safe aspect: staff training

This aspect describes the effectiveness of the school's online safety staff development programme and how it prepares and empowers staff to educate and intervene in issues when they arise.

Level 5	There is no planned online safety training programme for staff. Child Protection/Safeguarding training does not include online safety
Level 4	A planned online safety staff training programme is being developed, which aligns with Child Protection and Safeguarding training
Level 3	There is a planned programme of staff online safety training that is regularly revisited and updated. There is clear alignment and consistency with other Child Protection/Safeguarding training and vice versa. Training needs are informed through audits and the induction programme for new staff includes online safety. There is evidence that key members of staff (e.g. Online Safety Officer, Child Protection Officer, Data Officer) have received more specific training beyond general awareness raising. The Online Safety Officer can demonstrate how their own professional expertise has been sustained (e.g. through conferences, research, training or membership of expert groups)
Level 2	There is a planned programme of online safety training for all staff that is regularly revisited and updated. Staff are confident and informed in dealing with issues relating to their own personal well-being. There is clear alignment and consistency with other Child Protection/Safeguarding training (e.g. Prevent and vice versa). Training needs are informed through audits and the induction programme for new staff includes online safety. Where relevant, online safety training is included in Performance Management targets. There is evidence that key members of staff (e.g. Online Safety Officer, Child Protection Officer, Data Officer) have received more specific training beyond general awareness raising, some of which is accredited and recognised. The Online Safety Officer can demonstrate how their own professional expertise has been sustained and accredited
Level 1	There is a planned programme of online safety training for all staff that is regularly revisited and updated. Staff are confident and informed in dealing with issues relating to their own personal well-being. The school takes every opportunity to research and understand current good practice and training reflects this. There is clear alignment and consistency with other Child Protection/Safeguarding training (e.g. Prevent and vice versa). Training needs are informed through audits and the induction programme for new staff includes online safety. Where relevant, online safety training is included in Performance Management targets. There is evidence that key members of staff (e.g. Online Safety Officer, Child Protection Officer, Data Officer) have received more specific training beyond general awareness raising, some of which is accredited and recognised. The Online Safety Officer can demonstrate how their own professional expertise has been sustained and accredited. The culture of the school ensures that staff support each other in sharing knowledge and good practice about online safety. The impact of online safety training is evaluated and informs subsequent practice

Table 6.3 360 Degree Safe overall structure

Elements	Strands	Aspects
Policy and leadership	Responsibilities	E-safety group
		E-safety responsibilities
		Governors
	Policies	Policy development
		Policy scope
		Acceptable use agreement
		Self-evaluation
		Whole school
		Sanctions
		Reporting
	Communications and communication technologies	Mobile devices
		Social media
		Digital and video images
		Public online communications
		Professional standards
Infrastructure	Passwords	Password security
	Services	Connectivity and filtering
		Technical security
		Personal data
Education	Children and young people	E-safety education
		Digital literacy
		The contribution of young people
	Staff	Staff training
	Governors	Governor training
	Parents and carers	Parental education
	Community	Community engagement
Standards and inspection	Monitoring	Impact of e-safety policy and practice
		Monitoring the impact of the e-safety policy and practice

that eluded formal inspection. This certainly seems to have been the case in relation to the 360 Degree Safe project, as it tracks attitudes towards online safety, something that would be more difficult to record using alternative mechanisms.

As the practice of school self-review has become more established and nuanced over the years, Kyriakides and Campbell (2004) and Schildkampa et al. (2009) have argued that a strong set of evaluation criteria are the key to ensuring success and reliability. In the case of the

360 Degree Safe tool, a highly structured approach is used, suggesting that the data are likely to be sufficiently reliable for our purposes, namely assessing the changing attitudes of teachers and school administrators towards online safety. The provision of an inspection visit for schools that wish to apply for accreditation in online safety serves to enhance reliability and validity. However, it should be noted that schools that self-select for accreditation are more likely to have achieved maturity in their compliance processes. Nevertheless, such inspection visits during the life of the project (120 to date) have confirmed the school self-review data in each case, indicating that schools were generally accurate in their self-assessments about their online safety practices. To date this mechanism has not identified any anomalous scores —schools are generally consistent and honest with their ratings. It might be argued that, given the tool is intended for development and improvement purposes, it is not in the school's interest to inflate their scores.

As the tool continues to become more widespread, with increasing numbers of schools involved, reliability increases. As a final measure of validity, it should be noted that the database is analysed every year which results in annual "state of the nation" reports, published by the SWGfL (e. g. Phippen 2010; 2012a; 2013; 2014). In each of these cases, while there is overall improvement in aspects, the "shape" of the data (see below) has remained consistent, even with the addition of new establishments every year. This would indicate a great deal of validity of the data—the early adopters certainly did not present a different overall profile to those who are just starting to use the tool now.

The main focus of the analysis presented below is on how schools currently perform and what the implications are of this for online safety education and knowledge development for young people. In addition the tool allows for an overall analysis of aspect performance across the whole dataset, as well as providing a focus on specific aspects, regions and times.

Establishments Analysed

Annual analysis of the database takes place in September, therefore the analysis below draws on a data snapshot taken at the end of September 2015. The following discussion is drawn from this analysis, which can be

Table 6.4 Database baseline figures in September 2015

Establishments signed up to the tool on 30 September 2015	6950
Establishments which have embarked on the self-review process	4507
Establishments with full profiles completed	2834

Table 6.5 Establishment regions

Channel Islands	29
London	623
Midlands	1497
North East	597
North West	848
Overseas	18
South East	1187
South West	1816

Table 6.6 Establishment type

All through	25
Not applicable	154
Nursery	39
Primary	4590
Secondary	2142

explored in more detail in Phippen (2015). Table 6.4 shows the baseline statistics for establishment registrations at this time.

In considering the dataset from England, we can see a fair geographic distribution across the whole country. While the origins of the tool lie in the South West, it is clearly now a national tool, as illustrated in Table 6.5.

The "overseas" establishments that are registered generally comprise service schools abroad which are still considered part of the UK educational establishment profile. A number of establishments also didn't specify a location, which is why the total for location does not add up to the full 6950. However, as an indicator of geographical spread of establishments, we can see there is broad engagement across the country as a whole.

We can also consider the establishments registered in terms of phase, as shown in Table 6.6. Unsurprisingly there is mainly a split between primary and secondary schools, with the majority being primaries. The "not applicable" establishments are such entities as special schools, local authorities, informal education providers and the like.

ACTIVITY ON 360 DEGREE SAFE

It is not necessary for an establishment to have completed a full review of all 28 aspects to have their data logged and therefore available for analysis in the tool. In total, 2834 establishments from our population carried out the full self-review, and a further 4507 schools reviewed at least one aspect. In considering the use of the tool, one useful illustration is to measure activity in the tool over time—as an aggregation of activity across all users. This is shown in Fig. 6.1, where we can see a clear pattern of activity in each school year, with peaks in activity when returning at the start of the summer holidays and also after the Christmas break. What we can also see very clearly from this analysis is that activity on the tool has grown significantly over the years, particularly from the second half of 2012. As discussed above in September 2012, OFSTED included

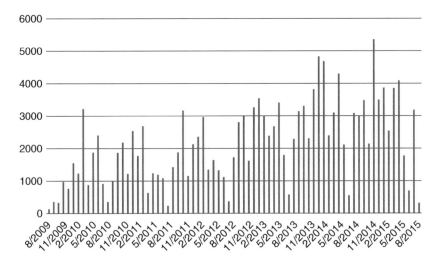

Fig. 6.1   Activity per month

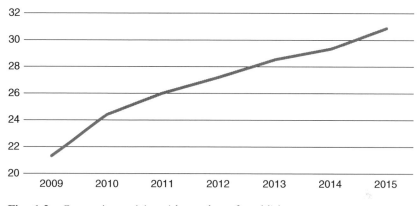

Fig. 6.2 Comparing activity with number of establishments

references to online safety within their Inspection Handbook explicitly for the first time.

The evidence presented certainly shows far more activity in recent years, though that does not necessarily mean that the tool is used more, just that there are more people using it. However, we can do a more detailed examination of this if we compare the number of establishments using the tool with the number of posts to the tool (i.e. the number of times an establishment has submitted either a new review of a given aspect, or revised one) per year, where we can clearly see an increase in activity over time.

As can be seen in Fig. 6.2, in 2010 each establishment using the tool would, on average, make 25 submissions. In 2015 that has increased to 31 submissions. So we can certainly suggest that establishments are making more use of the tool as it has embedded in the educational landscape and, arguably, the schools inspectorate places more importance on online safety policy and practice.

ANALYSIS OF THE DATASET: STATE OF THE NATION 2015

Moving on to the actual aspects themselves, and the overall performance across the whole dataset, a "state of the nation" analysis applies basic statistical measures to the database to get an overall picture of the data to allow us to understand where online safety policy and practice is, in general, across the country. Of course, we can only measure the performance of schools who

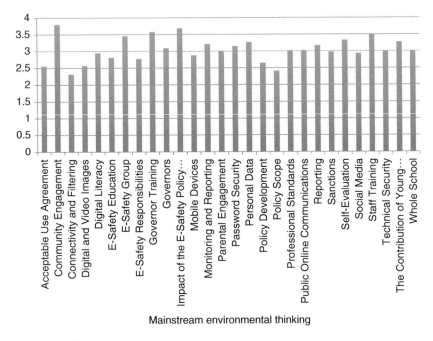

Fig. 6.3   Average rating per aspect

have engaged with the tool and we would hypothesise that those who have decided to adopt 360 Degree Safe into school self-review practice would be more committed to online safety than those who have yet to use it—a school with little interest in this area is unlikely to engage with the tool.

As discussed above, each aspect can be rated by the self-reviewing establishments on a progressive maturity scale from 5 (lowest rating) to 1 (highest), and each establishment can update their scores as they "improve," based on school improvement planning and implementation which can be drawn from the tool. Therefore, in order to determine national performance, average scores for each aspect are drawn from the lowest, or "best," rating given by each establishment. Fig. 6.3 illustrates overall averages across aspects.

From this initial analysis, we can see a range of average ratings across the different aspects of online safety policy and practice. Given that the lower the rating of each aspect, the stronger the performance, we can see strength in areas such as "connectivity and filtering," "acceptable usage policy" and "policy scope," all of which are below a mean of 2.5, showing that, on average, schools either have these things in place or have them well established. However, other aspects, such as "community engagement" and "staff training," have values of over 3.5, so with these aspects we are looking, on average, at more basic practice, or that they are not in place at all.

More specifically, the strongest aspects are:

- Connectivity and filtering (2.309);
- Policy scope (2.406);
- Acceptable use agreement (2.554);
- Digital and video images (2.568);
- Policy development (2.642).

And the weakest are:

- Community engagement (3.799);
- Impact of the e-safety policy and practice (3.686);
- Governor training (3.574);
- Staff training (3.498);
- E-safety group (3.457).

So with this top level analysis we can see that, across the country, it is far more likely that schools will have strength in the policy areas, with four out of the five strongest aspects being drawn from these. So we can see that, at least, schools are starting to establish policy around online safety, showing that they are at least cognisant of the need for school governance around this area. The technical aspect of connectivity and filtering has remained the strongest aspect ever since the establishment of the tool, which we would suggest is no surprise given the fact that such provision is often delivered by a third party, and once in place requires few resources to manage.

Another useful statistical measure for considering the performance of schools is to consider the standard deviation across each aspect in the dataset. From the statistics in Fig. 6.4 we can see that, in some areas of strength, such as the "strongest" (connectivity and filtering) there is consistency of strength. With a low average rating and a narrow standard deviation we know that there is little variability in performance across

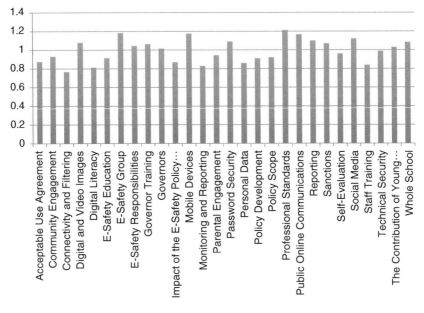

Fig. 6.4   Standard deviations per aspect

schools. We can also see a number of aspects where average performance is weaker and standard deviation is also narrow, suggesting consistent weaker performance. Perhaps the most concerning aspect here is staff training, with an average of 3.5 and a standard deviation of 0.82, which we could describe as consistently weak across the dataset. Community engagement, another very important aspect, which is the developing of the knowledge of other adult stakeholders in the online safety space, also shows a very low average and a fairly narrow standard deviation. Equally, if we look at an area such as mobile devices, which explores the quality of policy around the management of mobile devices in the school setting, we can see strength from the mean value (2.88) but with quite a broad standard deviation, which would suggest that some establishments are very strong in this area, where others are far weaker.

In drilling down to explore these distributions in more detail, we can also isolate each aspect per level, so we can quantify the proportion of establishments who have, for example, rated themselves 3 in staff training, or 4 in community engagement. Table 6.7 provides these statistics and can

Table 6.7 Aspect distribution per level

	1 (%)	2 (%)	3 (%)	4 (%)	5 (%)
Acceptable use agreement	8.24	43.48	35.03	11.15	2.09
Community engagement	0.89	4.80	35.47	31.15	27.68
Connectivity and filtering	13.71	46.41	35.22	4.56	0.10
Digital and video images	14.46	39.95	25.78	13.99	5.82
Digital literacy	2.29	26.18	48.92	19.93	2.68
E-safety education	4.95	34.98	38.01	18.71	3.36
E-safety group	4.26	22.12	19.81	31.28	22.53
E-safety responsibilities	11.75	31.77	26.17	28.63	1.69
Governor training	3.46	13.38	25.89	36.79	20.48
Governors	4.45	23.09	41.85	19.92	10.70
Impact of the e-safety policy and practice	1.28	6.61	30.66	45.13	16.32
Mobile devices	7.32	40.75	22.49	15.99	13.45
Monitoring and reporting on e-safety incidents	2.44	12.74	51.87	27.06	5.90
Parental engagement	3.58	28.26	38.15	24.68	5.32
Password security	6.28	20.91	37.36	22.31	13.14
Personal data	2.62	10.76	51.76	26.69	8.17
Policy development	8.85	37.26	36.65	15.37	1.87
Policy scope	11.58	52.86	20.94	12.67	1.95
Professional standards	8.07	35.26	16.96	26.57	13.14
Public online communications	7.58	31.98	23.04	25.39	12.01
Reporting	5.59	25.82	24.59	33.55	10.45
Sanctions	7.25	30.40	26.75	29.10	6.51
Self-evaluation	2.81	17.81	31.39	39.46	8.53
Social media	4.86	40.59	22.54	20.72	11.29
Staff training	2.22	7.37	37.37	44.52	8.53
Technical security	6.91	22.54	39.90	25.20	5.46
The contribution of young people	2.39	24.39	28.04	33.91	11.27
Whole school	6.61	29.52	30.05	24.68	9.13

even more clearly show the areas of concern for schools around online safety policy and practice.

This allows our most detailed exploration of the state of the nation. For example, there are good things that can be drawn from areas around policy and technology in place to protect young people from harmful content:

- 60 % of schools have excellent or good connectivity and filtering in place;
- Over 50 % have a detailed and effective acceptable usage agreement in place;

- Almost 50 % have strong practice around the management of mobile devices.

However, there are also statistics from this analysis that can cause grave concern:

- Almost 60 % of schools have no engagement with the community on online safety issues;
- 55 % have carried out no governor training around online safety issues;
- Over 50 % have no staff training to date around online safety;
- 30 % have no governor involvement in the development of online safety policy or practice.

Given we are analysing this data to, as the chapter title suggests, determine the gulf between adult stakeholders and the young people that we hope they are educating and protecting around online safety risks, the level of poor practice described above is cause for concern. Firstly, over 50 % of establishments in the 360 Degree Safe database have delivered no staff training around online safety—when we are looking to schools to ensure education in this area, how can we expect that to be effective if staff are not trained effectively?

Perhaps more concerning is the lack of governor engagement with online safety. As discussed elsewhere in this text, since the academy programme was rolled out across the country, which decoupled local authority scrutiny from schools, governors represent perhaps the only challenge to school leaders outside of the inspectorate. If governors are not conversant around the issues of online safety, how can they provide an effective challenge?

Comparing Primary and Secondary Establishments

Given the variability in practice from the whole dataset, a further decomposition of primary and secondary schools is logical. Due to the nature of education in these two phases, I have observed a lot a variation in practice between primary and secondary schools I visit—secondary schools will generally look at delivering "online safety education" in tutorial time or specific information and computing technology (ICT)/ personal, social health and economic education (PSHE) classes, whereas in primary settings there is

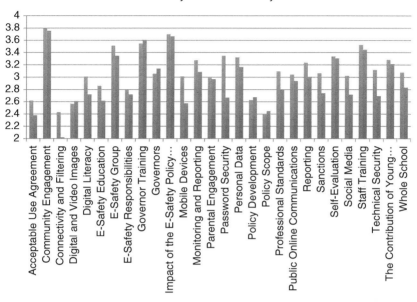

Fig. 6.5 Primary/secondary comparison 2015

more flexibility in the school timetable to deliver across subjects. I have also seen a more resistant attitude in some primary schools to addressing some of the more difficult aspects of online safety—particularly things like social media (the belief being they are all under the age of 13 therefore there is no need to address it) and those related to sex and relationships.

Looking at the 2015 dataset, we can certainly see some difference between the two phases of school (Fig. 6.5).

The first point to note is that, with this comparison, the "shape" of the data remains the same—while there are some variations between primary and secondary settings, the peaks (weaknesses) and troughs (strengths) are generally in the same places. However, if we focus on specific aspects, we can see some clear differences (Table 6.8).

It is interesting to note that policy scope is the strongest aspect in primary schools, stronger even that connectivity and filtering (which is considerably lower than the secondary average, even though it is still one of the strongest aspects). We can also see that mobile devices, or policy around them in the school, is stronger in secondary schools. This does

Table 6.8   Comparison of primary and secondary strengths

Primary strongest	Secondary strongest
Policy scope (2.396)	Connectivity and filtering (2.018)
Connectivity and filtering (2.429)	Acceptable use agreement (2.378)
Digital and video images (2.563)	Policy scope (2.447)
Acceptable use agreement (2.615)	Mobile devices (2.572)
Policy development (2.626)	Digital and video images (2.607)

Table 6.9   Primary and secondary weakest aspects

Primary weakest	Secondary weakest
Community engagement (3.801)	Community engagement (3.749)
Impact of the e-safety policy and practice (3.695)	Impact of the e-safety policy and practice (3.663)
Governor training (3.545)	Governor training (3.604)
Staff training (3.524)	Staff training (3.445)
E-safety group (3.512)	E-safety group (3.348)

suggest the view that mobile devices are something that primary schools need not consider, as they do not expect their pupils to have them in school. However, looking at the data from the survey in Chap. 3, as well as the OFCOM media literacy tracker (OFCOM 2014), this assumption might need to be challenged (Table 6.9).

For the weakest aspects, the order to aspects is the same in both settings, and while there are differences in averages (with primary schools being weaker in all but governor training), the differences tend to be less pronounced than among strengths.

In comparing distribution across different aspects (as explored in Table 6.7 with the full dataset), and then phases, space in this format means a presentation of the full dataset would be cumbersome and confusing. However, we can draw out comparisons on those where there is significant difference in the distributions, and this is detailed in Table 6.10.

From this comparison, we can draw the following conclusions:

- Almost 35 % of primary schools have no policy around mobiles;

Table 6.10 Comparison of aspects between primary and secondary schools

	1 (%)	2 (%)	3 (%)	4 (%)	5 (%)
Acceptable use agreement (p)	7.75	40.76	36.30	12.65	2.54
Acceptable use agreement (s)	9.07	52.12	31.25	7.06	0.50
Community engagement (p)	0.58	4.12	35.87	33.42	26.01
Community engagement (s)	1.78	7.57	34.56	26.15	29.94
Connectivity and filtering (p)	9.27	44.18	40.92	5.59	0.04
Connectivity and filtering (s)	24.25	51.51	22.52	1.62	0.11
Digital literacy (p)	2.00	23.51	48.94	22.73	2.82
Digital literacy (s)	3.22	35.10	49.83	10.24	1.61
E-safety education (p)	4.05	34.41	36.76	21.45	3.33
E-safety education (s)	7.28	38.52	42.38	9.27	2.54
Governor training (p)	3.26	13.96	25.88	38.80	18.10
Governor training (s)	4.63	13.05	25.27	31.44	25.62
Impact of the e-safety policy and practice (p)	0.98	6.24	30.39	47.11	15.28
Impact of the e-safety policy and practice (s)	2.03	6.69	32.97	39.55	18.76
Mobile devices (p)	5.06	38.44	22.71	17.83	15.95
Mobile devices (s)	12.00	45.41	23.70	11.17	7.72
Monitoring and reporting (p)	1.82	11.02	51.05	30.29	5.82
Monitoring and reporting (s)	3.25	15.78	55.45	20.30	5.22
Password security (p)	3.09	16.58	38.20	26.69	15.44
Password security (s)	14.42	31.26	35.47	10.95	7.89
Social media (p)	7.81	44.94	23.21	15.82	8.23
Social media (s)	3.73	38.39	22.56	22.71	12.61
Staff training (p)	1.53	6.41	37.78	46.65	7.62
Staff training (s)	3.08	10.05	37.44	38.13	11.30
Technical security (p)	4.90	18.68	42.05	28.48	5.88
Technical security (s)	11.37	33.07	34.33	17.34	3.90

Note: p = primary; s = secondary.

- Over 50 % of secondary schools have a strong policy around mobile devices;
- Over 40 % of primary schools have only basic filtering in place, with 6 % still not having any;
- 54 % of staff in primary schools have received no staff training around online safety;
- 30 % of secondary schools do nothing with the community related online safety matters;
- There are no secondary schools who demonstrate aspirational or innovating practice in engagement with the wider community;

- In both phases over 50 % of schools have no form of governor training around online safety in place;
- Schools place more effort on parental engagement compared to staff professional development.

CONVERSATIONS WITH EDUCATION PROFESSIONALS: DOING THEIR BEST IN THE FACE OF APATHY?

The 360 Degree Safe analysis in particular highlights the size of the gulf between young people's knowledge and practice around online issues, and the awareness of this by their teachers; and while there is evidence to show areas of strength, there are also many areas of concern. However, it would be churlish to suggest that it is the fault of teaching staff. In the following section, I will explore in more depth my own experiences working in schools with teachers and reflect on a profession which, in general, knows it needs to do something in this area, but with little guidance from either senior management or national policy, and often feels it is doing "anything" other than what is actually needed.

From my own experiences with children and young people, the most common question I get asked at the end of a session, particularly if it is a workshop/discussion group, rather than just an assembly (which has its place but rarely allows young people to ask questions or really engage in discussion around a topic) is "When are you coming back?"

This has happened to me many times, from children of all ages. And when I ask why they want me to come back, the general reason is "We never get a chance to talk about this sort of thing."

There certainly seems to be an expectation among young people that teachers within their school will have a prohibitive approach to online safety, whether this is at a secondary school where I am told by young people that disclosing an issue around sexting, upsetting material or abuse will result in a telling off, or in a primary school where the children are told to stay off social media. I have visited many primary schools and the ethos at some is that there is no reason to talk about Instagram, Facebook and other forms of social media with the pupils because "they shouldn't be on it." However, when asked by those who have a prohibitive perspective on social media why there is this "rule" that there should be no under 13s on it, very few are aware of the real reasons for it—most assume there are child protection reasons.

As a counter to this I would draw on the wisdom of a 14-year-old girl I spoke to about where online safety should be delivered in the curriculum, and her views on her primary school, whose staff think they don't have to address online safety education. Her response was simply: "It's like saying we shouldn't have to do sex education until we're actually having sex."

There seem to be constant demands on teachers to cover all manner of different social education within the curriculum, from whichever pressure group or lobby that seems to view their own passion as the most important aspect of social education for children. However, with online safety, the pressure doesn't just come from pressure groups and academics such as myself—there are now clear demands from the inspectorate and from within the wider curriculum. In addition, policy direction, and the reactive media, all focus very clearly on a specific aspect of "safety" (i.e. inappropriate content). If we refer to the metrics associated with the 360 Degree Safe tool, the breadth of online safety is clear, and there is a great deal of guidance within the tool on how to develop a whole school approach to safety. However, engagement with this tool is voluntary and does not specifically have to be adopted as an improvement tool.

Coupled with this frustration by many teaching staff I speak to is the concern of a lack of support from senior management. Within the majority of school settings I visit there are usually one or two staff who have been tasked with "leading" on online safety. Sometimes this is because they are an ICT lead in the school and the senior leaders and/or governors have decided this is the place to fit in online safety, or sometimes because they have just shown an interest in the area. This may be because they are a parent and have had conversations with their own children about their behaviours and wish to learn more, because they are concerned about online issues, because they see it as a promotion opportunity, or because they are genuinely engaged in the area. Returning to the linkage between ICT and online safety in schools, this is something I often see. It is also one I find unusual, which I assume is a result of my work in the area. While there might be a superficial link between the two (ICT is used in the interactions that cause the need for online safety), the issues around online safety are usually related to behaviours, safeguarding, risk and well-being. While technology is part of the mix in terms of building resilience in online situations, it is not the driving aspect. As a colleague of mine is often heard to say in talks: "Putting online safety into ICT lessons is a little like putting drugs awareness in the science class."

I recall one conversation with a head of ICT who was appointed as "online safety lead" for their school, but told very specifically to stay away from topics such as sexting because "If we start talking about these things in school it might encourage them to do it."

I have a certain amount of sympathy with this position, particularly as school leaders often have to face questioning by parents about difficult issues. However, these sensitivities will often arise from the fact that the focus is on the act rather than the underlying behaviours. For example, if schools say that they are going to deliver a lesson on "sexting" to a group of year 7 pupils, it might be understandable that parents, not immersed in the world of online safety, would react badly to this, saying that it would just encourage these sort of practices. However, if the school was to talk about doing lessons on "respect, boundaries and esteem, using online issues as a vehicle to explore these," they might be met with less hostility.

I would suggest that, in some cases, the refusal to address education around these topics in the primary setting is less to do with concern regarding legal barriers than the fact that the knowledge of the teachers themselves is not sufficient enough to be able to deliver teaching on the topic effectively. Therefore it is easier for the school to say "they shouldn't be on it," rather than acknowledging that, regardless of in school policing, some pupils are using these sites, this is not going to change, and the potential issues that arise on these sites may spill into issues of well-being and safeguarding of children in the school, therefore it would be more proactive to educate children on safe use, rather than apply a prohibitive policy.

I was recently asked by a boy in a primary school what I thought of young people his age who used social media. I said to him that, before I answered, I'd be interested to hear his views on the topic. He provided a very mature answer that he couldn't see what they were doing wrong, as long as they were sensible, only communicated with people they knew and made sure their privacy settings were strong. I found it difficult to disagree.

By contrast, I have often been told by teachers of children of all ages that "they know more than we do" about social media. While I might agree that in some cases young people are highly proficient in the use of social media platforms, mobile devices, gaming platforms and all manner of other online technology, they have far less experience in, for example, understanding risk, safeguarding, well-being, counselling and pastoral care, and incident management. I would acknowledge that, if we focus online safety education entirely on the technological aspects of safety and safeguarding, teachers are unlikely to be as immersed in this world as much as the pupils at their school. However, the risk always with chasing technology is that you are only ever going to address symptoms, rather than root causes. The issues that arise with social media are rarely platform dependent —as raised by the discussion in Chap. 3 when exploring what young people say upsets them online, which is people, not platforms. And if teachers and senior leaders in schools are adopting prohibitive approaches, they will never get the opportunity to develop this deeper understanding of the issues around online safety and safeguarding children online.

With a lack of knowledge among the staff base, and a growing pressure to do this elusive "something," the schools will often fall back on the support of outside providers. However, I am told, the quality of these providers is variable and it can be difficult to judge what makes a good external provider. Again, with little national coordination or any form of quality mark (outside of the reputations of the organisations they represent), virtually anyone can set themselves up as an "online safety expert" and deliver education in schools, especially if the teaching staff do not have effective knowledge to inform their judgement on whether the providers are themselves knowledgeable or providing an effective level of education.

As I have already mentioned, another area of pressure around the need to do "something" is the changes in inspection frameworks by OFSTED over the past five years. I have highlighted how the changes in the frameworks in 2012 can be observed in the 360 Degree Safe tool, with considerably more registrations and activity once these changes had been announced. What is less clear to evidence is whether the inspection pressure has resulted in better education. Certainly more schools are trying to do this elusive "something" around online safety since changes were made in the inspection framework. However, I am sure I am not the only visitor to schools who has been asked things such as: "Can you come in and do an assembly, we've OFSTED coming soon?"

Discussions with senior leaders are often very honest about the scrutiny they face—with the focus of inspection, league tables and other external judges of quality being on academic achievement, this is where their efforts have lain in the last few years. While the inspection framework is now changing to ask specific questions around online safety and with more of a focus on spiritual, moral, social and cultural education (OFSTED 2015), senior leaders will still see the driving factors behind inspection being academic success and delivering on statutory curricula. Given that there is little assessment, in academic terms, around online safety, and that neither personal, social and health education nor sex and relationship education are compulsory subjects in English schools (outside of the need to teach the biology of reproduction), it cannot come as too much of a surprise that they aren't the top of the list of priorities for many senior leaders in schools.

We can see that when these issues are explicitly addressed within an inspection, this can have an impact on the school, and also on neighbouring establishments. In a recent inspection of a school in the South West of England, judgements on the school, particularly around safeguarding, were particularly damning, and raised concerns around online issues such as "a culture of sexting was prevalent and accepted as typical" (BBC 2015b).

While this inspection was clearly damaging to the school at the time, what can be observed around the wider schools network is that this impact has resulted in more commitment to issues around online safety. A number of safeguarding leads in neighbouring schools have told me that there seems to be a renewed vigour by the senior management around online safety as a direct result of the published inspection report. Therefore, we can certainly report observations linking the impact of inspection that are cognisant of online safety issues with improved practice.

However, I should stress that, while I have discussed a fairly negative image around this "gulf" between young people and adult stakeholders, this is not always the case. I have visited schools that have online safety delivered across the curriculum, looking at it from a holistic perspective and something that is engaged with by staff and students alike and where young people do have respect for their teachers knowledge and have the opportunity to discuss such issues in class. This isn't to say that the teachers are particularly technology savvy, just that they recognise their knowledge and experience as teaching professionals can help the young people in their care develop resilience and coping strategies around online issues, rather than being told the latest settings on a given social media platform or the new legislation around sexting.

What is usually apparent from these schools is that the whole school community is engaged with the topic, starting from the head teacher and governors and disseminating across the school. That is not to say that these schools are not without online safety incidents, in fact, they acknowledge that they will happen; but they can support young people because they have developed a proactive incident response, rather than refusing to accept this as a possibility.

In drawing this chapter to a close, I am mindful of two key issues that arise from exploring the capabilities of education professionals to address the challenges of online safety for their schools and their pupils.

Firstly, this is an area that is quite simply crying out for national coordination, around curriculum, leadership and governance. Teachers need permission to engage with the issues around online safety in schools, and to place importance on it. But they also need to know what they might do, rather than being left to their own devices to do this elusive "something." However, it would seem that those who could make positive change in this direction are still resistant (Morgan 2016).

The second key issue is to move our understanding of online safety away from chasing technology and focus more on behaviours. If we are asking teachers to become more expert on the latest social media platforms and whatever social apps are most popular with young people at any given time, we are doomed to fail. However, when talking to young people about how they feel we could address these issues, they are very clear where more effective approaches should lie. They do not want to be told how to use technologies safely, they instead, in my experience, are asking for the following:

- An awareness of the legal and rights based issues around protection from harassment, consent, freedom of speech, and so on;
- An opportunity to engage in discussions around the topic, asking questions, across all manner of related issues;
- Knowing that if things do go wrong, they will be able to talk to someone without a judgemental, prohibitive perspective on what has happened (the last thing a young person who has become victim to, for example, a redistributed image of themselves needs to hear is "you shouldn't have done that");
- A willingness to engage in further discussion/education around the topics.

So, in returning to the title of this chapter, if we are going to consider the gulf to be that of knowledge of digital technologies and their use as it exists between young people and education professionals, then this gulf is wide. Perhaps if we continue with our constant need to place online issues in separate boxes, rather than trying to understand that these are interconnected risks and challenges that have existed for a very long time, but are just facilitated in different ways as a result of online technology, we will always have this gulf. It is unlikely, given the pressures of the job and the delivery of the core curriculum in the classroom, that teachers will exceed young people in the early adoption of new technology. But we should ask whether this is needed at all. In the final chapter of this text, we will explore this in more detail, and propose that with this focus, particularly from the policy area, we will always be doomed to fail. We need to develop a deeper understanding of behaviours and adapt our metaphors to enable a more meaningful dialogue around this online safety area.

NOTE

1. https://360safe.org.uk/Files/Documents/School-E-SafetyV3). Accessed 1 May 2016.

CHAPTER 7

Where Next?

Abstract The gulf between adult and child stakeholders within the domain of child online safety can be significant, and this is highlighted when exploring issues such as gaming and sexting with young people when they are given the opportunity to discuss them in a supportive and non-judgemental manner. The author proposes that the safety metaphor is failing, mainly due to an increasingly narrow and unhelpful focus upon prevention rather than empowerment, education or understanding. He also argues that any "solution" that erodes children and young people's rights is no solution at all and suggests that, without an understanding of the root causes of online issues, and their relation to well-being and mental health, we will always fail to ensure they are "safe" online.

Keywords Child online safety · Children's rights · Education · Digital well-being

In this book we have explored the complexities of the relationships young people have with technology and how we might keep them safe when they are using it. While we started with an analysis of policy in the UK around this field, we have developed an argument that the current approaches are failing to address the complexities around how young people might use digital technology safely. In particular this is due to a focus on a single aspect of online safety—prohibition of access to

© The Author(s) 2017   131
A. Phippen, *Children's Online Behaviour and Safety*,
DOI 10.1057/978-1-137-57095-6_7

inappropriate content. However, in drawing from a rich evidence base of both quantitative and qualitative data, we have proposed a far more complex social context than a prohibitive ideology can ever hope to address.

Firstly, we have seen in Chap. 3 that young people have a highly absorbed relationship with technology—it permeates many aspects of their lives and they readily engage with it. They believe, in general, that they are knowledgeable about the potential risks and threats that exist, and they acknowledge that sometimes they are upset by things that happen online. Arguably, they also have a more mature perspective on what education might look like, and can be very honest about what they think of educational approaches and policy solutions when given the opportunity to discuss them. We have also seen that, as they get older, they become increasingly unlikely to turn to adults for help and advice.

In Chaps 4 and 5 we explored in depth two areas on concern around young people, namely gaming and sexting, and once again highlighted that, while content in gaming, and the act of sexting, may be the focus of public concern, by exploring these issues in depth, and drawing on the evidence, we can better understand the areas of risk and motivations for engaging in such risky behaviours.

In Chap. 6, we looked more closely at the education environment itself—firstly by exploring what we referred to as the "state of the nation" around online safety, and, through an analysis of the 360 Degree Safe database, highlighted that, while schools may be getting to grips with ensuring appropriate policy is in place to address online safety issues, the more complex aspects, such as ensuring staff and governors are up to date with their awareness of behaviours and risk, are less strong. We have also highlighted the challenges faced by education professionals in this space—without support from senior leaders, and with a lack of national coordination, they are in the position of knowing they need to do something, but what that something might be is less clear.

We have also suggested that, while there has been a great deal more policy activity in this area over the last five years, perhaps it does not acknowledge this complexity and has adopted a prohibitive ideology which may be counter-productive. So what might happen if we do nothing about this? If we accept a policy direction that seeks to prevent access to content, blame service providers for the issues that arise and fail to embrace a social policy that looks beyond the technical aspects of these phenomena, what might be the outcomes for society?

It seems that when it comes to online safety, we are still focusing on the delivery mechanism, rather than the underlying behaviours. I was recently asked if I could do a talk on "What the next 20 years of online safety will hold." My simple response was, if we are going to use technology as a focus, this was not possible. We struggle to understand how technology evolves and impacts on our social lives until it is "out there" and people are using it. Given young people's disruptive and often unpredictable use of technology, what may or may not be popular with this demographic is even more difficult to pre-empt.

If we do nothing, if we accept a prohibitive approach to online safety, and continue to expect industry to find all of the answers, "given they are the ones that caused these issues" (BBC 2013), the problems, risks, unsafe behaviours and abuse will continue to develop as technology facilitates more complex forms of social interaction and young people will not have the knowledge and coping mechanisms to be aware of what is and is not acceptable.

However, can industry always pre-empt, even with the support of self-review frameworks, what might occur with their technologies once released? For example, the prevalence of 4G mobile phones means that streaming video from a mobile device becomes far more common practice, as does the "selfie." And virtual reality headsets in gaming means interaction can happen on a far more complex level. How might two sexually aroused teens in separate homes use virtual reality headsets and a superfast broadband connection in the years to come? What might result in the interactions they have? Might they place themselves at risk of public exposure and have to deal with the resultant abuse? The true answer to this is we don't know, and if we try to pre-empt what might happen, I am sure we will fail to come up with a full and accurate set of scenarios.

I have, over my career, been extremely critical of industry, as there have certainly been times where safety and ethics have not been at the top of their list when it comes to deploying new technology. However, in more recent times I see industry really engaging with the online safety community, both within the UK and further afield. The UK Council for Child Internet Safety has strong representation from industry, and it is via industry, through subscription fees, that an organisation such as the Internet Watch Foundation exists. However, industry can only do so much on its own. While it is encouraging to note that children's rights are beginning to become part of the thinking around how technology is used, particularly in social settings, again the focus is on how industry should do more.

The expectation of industry around education is an interesting one, given that they have little capacity to reach children and young people in the same way that, for example, a school can. While they might be able to provide supporting materials to educate those using their products and services around the potential online risks, this has to remain "pulled" information—it requires the end user, be it child or adult, to actively look for the material, and read it.

Surely, the major focus for the knowledge development of these issues should be in school? However, we seem less concerned about the role of government in this complex issue. If it is the role of government to define legislature and policy across all areas of society, then they have a responsibility to provide education that is fit for purpose and addresses the concerns of growing up in a connected, online world. As the analysis in this text has highlighted, it would seem that while the policy has almost completely focussed on a single, specific aspect of online safety (access to inappropriate material) the needs of young people are far more complex, and the schools themselves are not sure, given the lack of national coordination, on how online safety should be addressed in the classroom. With the recent consultation on statutory guidance for safeguarding in schools, once again it seems that schools are being told they need to deliver education around online safety, yet they are not helped to do this with any guidance on what this might look like.

The prohibitive ideology does little to develop the knowledge of young people around these problems and certainly does nothing to help develop resilience or coping strategies to address changing behaviours and risks that have not yet been possible to analyse or predict. Put simply, if we aim to protect children from the perils of the Internet by making sure they are not exposed to them, what happens when we fail to achieve this, as we surely will? Even with the most prohibitive strategies at home, with all manners of filter and monitoring in place, could a parent ever be truly sure that their child will be unaffected by what is happening around them? As we have discussed in Chap. 6 around the comment by the parent who believed her child did not need any education on online safety "because they are not stupid," we need to acknowledge that, regardless of an individual child's own behaviour, he or she will be exposed to the behaviours of others.

We also need policy to be drawn from evidence, rather than gut feeling and moral panic. As discussed in Chap. 4, it is too easy to "decide" something is harmful without any foundation in evidence. During my engagement with various adult stakeholders in this area, I find it interesting that, regardless of position and role within this field, many professionals will still revert to being a parent or grandparent, rather than maintaining an objective perspective. I can recall a discussion with a high court judge about my work, and its relationship to the legal process, when suddenly he produced his mobile phone and said "How quickly could you access pornography on this?" When I responded with "About two seconds, would you like me to show you?" his response was "So my granddaughter could be playing on my phone and see pornography? How can I stop this?"

It is easy to see why these prohibitive approaches manifest—when we hear of young people accessing pornography, exchanging indecent images or using horrifically abusive language toward each other, our first reaction, particularly if reflecting on the potential impact on our own children or grandchildren, is "How can I stop this?" However, taking this approach perhaps will only address a factor in causing harm, rather than the root cause.

A potentially wider social impact of not doing anything different is that a generation engaging with technology in potentially risky ways is moving on from an education system that has ill prepared them for what is acceptable and unacceptable into adult society and the workplace (Phippen and Ashby 2014). Do we risk producing a generation whose behaviours clash with what we may expect of mature members of society, and are we comfortable with how we may address this? We are already seeing companies struggling with how to respond to social digital practices in the workplace and they cannot assume that new employees will be fully aware of the implications of digital social behaviours. Certainly recent case law based around the Serious Crime Bill's "revenge porn" legislation (UK Government 2015a) would show that such irresponsible and harmful behaviours hardly stop at the age of 18. It would seem, as already discussed in previous chapters, that digital technology provides us with a buffer against what we might view as "normally" socially acceptable, due to issues such as the lack of empathy, not seeing the impact of actions, the perceived anonymity of the act, and so on.

In practical terms, we might argue that the experience of these technologies suggests that it is time for a revised education and social policy that deals more effectively with matters such as Internet safety and safeguarding. However, perhaps most importantly, effective social and sex and relationship education is needed that embraces the blurred boundaries between online and offline interaction rather than compartmentalising the curriculum and judging education success based upon examination results.

From my experiences, one of the most surprising things for me is talking to someone who can see nothing wrong with asking someone for an explicit image or saying, for example, that they "hope their gran gets AIDS." This doesn't mean they are bad people, or in some way growing up uncontrolled and deviant. It does, however, mean that they are experiencing these things with their peers and have never had the opportunity to learn about the implications of these things or the impact that words (or abuse) can have on individuals.

Young people are asking for the opportunity to talk about these issues at school, but we are not providing them with safe, non-judgemental environments with which to do this. We seem to assume they should magically know that such behaviour is unacceptable and that, if we can control their use of technology, we will ensure they never behave in such a way. When I have challenged groups of teenage males about them knowing people who, as a way of trying to commence a relationship with someone, take an image of their genitals and send it to the target of their affections, sometimes their looks of bewilderment express more than their words. Sometimes they even say "Isn't that how a relationship starts?" And who would blame them for thinking this if the only conversations they have ever had about relationships are with their peers, and they see media stories with celebrities conducting such practices?

We can learn far more about how to address these issues from listening to young people, rather than judging them on their mistakes as they grow up. Yet they seem to remain the silent stakeholder in this area—a group who have policy, lessons and judgement forced upon them, rather than being spoken to about how they feel online safety should be addressed.

I have learned more from talking to young people about their online lives than I ever have in discussions, round-table debates and conferences held by practitioners, policy makers, academics or industry in this field. That is not to say all of the stakeholders have nothing to say, of course they do, which is why we should view this whole field as one comprising of multiple stakeholder groups. However, the evidence base from which they draw will generally be incomplete and lack the richness of experience compared to those who are actually living this life every day.

I was inspired to start this book by a comment from a 15-year-old girl I had the pleasure of spending a week with last year as part of her school work experience activity. If I have merely extended her comment, it would seem, once again, that young people have a far more mature grasp on some of these issues than some in the adult population.

> When telling some of my friends and family about this project, one of the things I constantly found myself saying is that I want people to understand properly what teenagers are experiencing. All of my friends have agreed that they feel mental health and body image are two of the most important issues they are facing or feel are being faced by their peers, yet these issues are two of the most unnoticed and disregarded problems.
>
> So the underlying question is how this can be solved. The truth is, we are never going to be able to filter the media and Internet to the extent of keeping everyone safe and happy and quite frankly we will never ever be able to filter "real life." So I believe the solution lies in teaching and helping young people to cope with the content on both the Internet and in the media, and to teach young people how to be more bodily and mentally confident. It will take time and effort on everyone's part, but I think it's clear that these are no longer things that can be brushed under the carpet but problems that are now well and truly in the spotlight.

As I stated in Chap. 1, one of the fundamental aspects of the ethnography of this research has been my own journey as a researcher in this field. My views now are very different from the ones I had back in 2010. And the major facilitator of the change of these views has been conversations with young people. The week I spent with this young lady was extremely challenging to my own preconceptions around this field. I was initially surprised, when she asked to do work experience with me, that she said she wanted to focus on body image. I had worked with her year group in her school before and the focus had always been on their relationship with digital technology—how it impacted on their lives and how they might reduce risk and mitigate against harm. When I asked her why, given the work I'd done in class with her in the past, she thought she might be able to relate body image and mental health to this area: she was extremely clear that of course they were related because the online world is the key contributing factor to issues of body image and the resultant mental health issues. Of course, she said, young people have issues around body image as a result of the online world—they are exposed to stereotypical perspectives of beauty via online media channels, YouTube celebrities get famous by giving glamour advice, peers post up photographs of what they deem to be attractive, and the social media world connects all young people together so that judgements on body image can span far beyond the school boundaries.

With my "safety" view of the world, particularly how we might provide education for young people so they can engage with online technologies in a "safe" manner, I was missing the wider perspective on all of this—what we are really talking about here is well-being and mental resilience.

So perhaps we have been getting the very nature of online safety wrong. As I was asked by a 10-year-old boy very recently: Can you ever make anything safe anyway? In which case, does the safety metaphor actually restrict our understanding of what it is like to grow up in the digital world? If we are truly going to "properly understand what teenagers are experiencing" then is safety the correct approach? It would seem, looking back on the comparison of the OFSTED and House of Lords definitions of Online Safety (see Chap. 2), there isn't really even any agreement on what different parts of the education regulatory process understand by the term. If those setting policy and conducting inspection cannot agree, then how can we hope for schools to be able to embrace effectively the broad range of issues affecting young people's lives through digital technology? While the 360 Degree Safe tool defines a broad standard around online safety, this does not seem to be reflected in the formation of policy. Perhaps reflecting on experiences from a well-being or even mental health perspective is far more productive if we are to move away from a prohibitive ideology.

Issues related to the abuse and behaviours we have explored have illustrated that, while online environments might be the places in which abuse is delivered, the nature of the abuse can vary and really is not anything particularly novel as a result of the technology involved. Within this text we have explored various issues around the nature of abuse and the rationales of "risky" online behaviour, such as:

- Self-esteem;
- Attention seeking;
- Legitimisation;
- Normalisation;
- Peer validation;
- Bullying and victimisation.

With all of these things we can see issues of empathy, peer respect and a lack of emotional intelligence playing a part—a lot of the types of abuse we have explored arise from a lack of thought about the impact of actions or the self-esteem of the content creator—the technological delivery of a lot of the abuse can extend the disconnect between abuser and victim.

In these cases, while some technological approaches might provide some level of intervention, such as monitoring to identify potentially abusive communication, the heart of these issues falls far beyond digital intermediations.

Similarly, if we consider a "technological phenomenon" such as sexting, I am reminded of the comment from the 14-year-old boy: "Popular girls don't sext." If we are to look objectively at the issues around sexting, the act is just a manifestation of all manner of social factors, such as esteem, the need to be popular (and an indication of popularity is being in a relationship), peer pressure, respect, boundaries and consent.

There is an urgent need to develop an education environment for children to be able to navigate through the complexity of a connected world. They need to be able to ask questions and ask for help in a supportive, non-judgemental environment. In turn, this needs to be supported by policy, practice and national coordination that acknowledges, rather than shies away from, the issues arising from growing up in the twenty-first century.

While content is clearly an issue, technology will only ever be a tool, not a solution, to addressing the fall out from the harm that might result. Assuming that, given filtering and monitoring is in place, there is little need to tackle why someone might be upset by a given type of content, whereas another young person might view it as humorous and be able to shrug off its potentially harmful effects. Young people need fora to discuss such things and know that if they are exposed to content that has upset them, they will not be scolded as "they shouldn't have been looking at that sort of thing". We will never totally prevent young people from accessing content we might consider to be, and indeed can be, inappropriate and harmful to them. But if the educational approach is prohibitive, then where does a young person turn if he or she is harmed? We can see from the discussion in earlier chapters that, particularly once in their teenage years, young people are far more likely to turn to a peer than a supportive adult regarding these issues, which potentially means the issue will be less likely to be resolved.

We need to explore motivations and justifications for these behaviours, we need to understand how we might build resilience not just to address these problems, but to help ensure when such issues arise (e.g. a child getting a request from another to send them an explicit selfie) that young people are aware they can say no and can disclose it has happened, and also, most importantly, make them aware of these sorts of acts in the first place. Not talking about sexting in secondary schools will not prevent it from happening, just as not talking about social media in primary schools will not prevent some of the children from using it.

So in conclusion, what will happen if we do nothing to change the direction we are headed? We will certainly ensure that some children don't access inappropriate material, and schools may identify a number of their pupils who are trying to access websites that their software has deemed inappropriate. And in a minority of homes, parents may have prevented one route to pornography. However, we might also be failing them in their right to an effective, relevant education and the right to be able to access useful information. In short, this preventative ideology is failing to deliver on young people's rights while trying to protect them from the "darkest corners of the Internet."

Young people want education in this area. Why are we not providing it for them? Perhaps it because our own prejudices, gut reactions and fears are preventing an effective dialogue from taking place. It is far easier for a politician to say "Children are looking at pornography, we must stop this," rather than the more complex "Children are looking at pornography and while we can't stop this we can provide tools that might mitigate exposure and put education in place where they might discuss what might result from exposure to pornography while providing a safe environment for them to disclose whether they have any fears of concerns about this." And indeed, there is probably a heavy public expectation for a "solution" to these issues.

Equally, I have a great deal of respect for the teachers I have worked with over these last few years, and can sympathise with them about the dilemma they face around online safety. Teachers fear for their jobs, and without national coordination on these issues, who can blame them? A teacher who takes it upon him or herself to address concerns about pornography or sexting within a classroom session, without effective training or knowledge of the area, and without the support of senior management or governors, risks that classic parental outrage than might result in a child from that class going home to say "My teacher talked to me about pornography today." While the Department of Education places responsibility for safeguarding in this area on the board of governors or "proprietors" it does little to detail what this safeguarding might be, how the school might provide education or what these levels of responsibility are, other than to ensure "appropriate" filtering and monitoring is in place while, at the same time, telling them to ensure that restrictive over blocking does not take place! If over blocking is an issue not resolved after 15 years of filtering in schools, I have little faith that school governors can find the solution.

However, if we were to align online issues alongside established child welfare and safeguarding, rather than presenting it as another thing they need to address through technological intervention, perhaps it would seem less daunting to education professionals. A teenager exposed to pornography resulting in issues such as size and performance anxieties is surely a child welfare issue, in the same way that a child being bullied via social media is. While our gut reaction to a teen saying they're worried about a friend looking at too much pornography might be to say "Well tell them not to do it then," or our response to a victim of sexting saying they are being bullied to the point that they do not want to get up in the morning is to say "Well perhaps you should not have done it then," we are, essentially, dealing with vulnerable children who deserve more than judgement and self-righteousness.

And we also need to acknowledge parents' fears in this area. As Livingstone et al. (2011) has raised, it is a difficult thing to hear that one's child is becoming sexually aware or engaging in what we might, as parents, view as inappropriate behaviour. And from this perspective, we can appreciate that there is parental opposition to education around sex and relationships. However, as raised in the Education Select Committee report (Education Select Committee 2015), if we refocus sex and relationship education (SRE) as "RSE," with the focus not on sex, but on relationships, one would hope that there would be less opposition.

One key issue that can be drawn from all of my discussions with young people, and one I have raised several times through this book, is that they are calling out for effective education in this area, but are not receiving it. And, as can be seen from the quote from my work experience colleague, they can already see the links between digital behaviour and well-being: it is other stakeholders, with their more prohibitive perspectives and short-term "fixes," that do not.

At the start of this book, I highlighted that, while the focus would be on online safety policy in the UK, because, from an ethnographic perspective, that was the field of analysis, this is not specifically a UK issue. This exploration has been a case study of dealing with complex social issues involving children and how governments and other stakeholders go about trying to prevent harm. While I have argued, in some places quite strongly, that the UK policy approach is wrong, it is not out of line with other approaches which equally hope that prevention results in changes in behaviour. However, regardless of geography, we can apply international treaties such as the UN Convention on the Rights of the Child as a framework for helping us to understand when we help and empower children, and when we hinder them, in our efforts to make them safer and free from harm. It is encouraging to see that the treaty is increasingly being applied to the space, and I would hope that by refocussing efforts away from prohibition toward more inclusive, well-being oriented strategies, a rights based perspective will prove to be extremely useful.

As we move forward in this area, and as new technologies develop, there will be further challenges to young people's rights and an increased need to provide effective education so they can engage with whatever is ahead of us, while mitigating risk. And while we may feel that our approaches to making them safe are the correct ones, we need always to remain mindful that a solution that provides a negligible degree of safety at the expense of, for example, education, privacy or expression is not really a solution at all.

REFERENCES

Al-Riyami, F. (2015). Microsoft Bing and Google's efforts to block child abuse searches are working. http://www.winbeta.org/news/microsoft-bing-and-googles-efforts-block-child-abuse-searches-are-working. Accessed 1 May 2016.

BBC. (2001). Columbine families sue computer game makers. http://news.bbc.co.uk/1/hi/sci/tech/1295920.stm. Accessed 1 October 2016.

BBC. (2004). Game blamed for hammer murder. http://news.bbc.co.uk/1/hi/england/leicestershire/3934277.stm. Accessed 1 May 2016.

BBC. (2015a). Heads' threat to parents over computer games. http://www.bbc.co.uk/news/uk-england-32103991. Accessed 1 May 2016.

BCC. (2015b). Callington College homophobia, racism and sexting probed by Ofsted. http://www.bbc.co.uk/news/uk-england-cornwall-31172802. Accessed 1 May 2016.

Billboard. (1982). "Custer" game is subject of two lawsuits. https://books.google.co.uk/books?id=8iMEAAAAMBAJ&pg=PT7&redir_esc=y#v=onepage&q&f=false. Accessed 1 May 2016.

Billington, J (2015). EU rules to make UK porn filters illegal—or so it thought. http://www.ibtimes.co.uk/eu-rules-make-uk-porn-filters-illegal-so-it-thought-1526314. Accessed 1 May 2016.

Boyd, D. (2014). *It's complicated: The social lives of networked teens.* New Haven: Yale University Press.

Byron, T. (2008). *Safer children in a digital world.* London: HMSO.

Byron (2010). "Do we have safer children in a digital world? A review of progress since the 2008 Byron Review". http://dera.ioe.ac.uk/709/7/do%20we%20have%20safer%20children%20in%20a%20digital%20world-WEB_Redacted.pdf. pg 7. Accessed Sept 2016.

© The Author(s) 2017
A. Phippen, *Children's Online Behaviour and Safety*,
DOI 10.1057/978-1-137-57095-6

Cameron, D. (2013, July 22). *The Internet and pornography: Prime Minister calls for action.* Speech to the National Society for the Prevention of Cruelty to Children. https://www.gov.uk/government/speeches/the-Internet-and-pornography-prime-minister-calls-for-action. Accessed 1 May 2016.

Cameron, D. (2014). #WeProtect children online global summit: Prime Minister's speech. https://www.gov.uk/government/speeches/weprotect-children-online-global-summit-prime-ministers-speech. Accessed 1 May 2016.

Caplan, S., Williams, D., & Yee, N. (2009). Problematic Internet use and psychosocial well- being among MMO players. *Computers in Human Behavior, 25*(6), 1312–1319.

Childwise. (2016). The monitor report 2016. http://www.childwise.co.uk/reports.html. Accessed 1 May 2016.

Clarke, L. (2014). Claire Perry: Ban phones in schools and turn off the router to protect children. http://www.wired.co.uk/news/archive/2014-01/29/claire-perry-overblocking-banning. Accessed 1 May 2016.

Crown Prosecution Service. (2015). Indecent images of children. http://www.cps.gov.uk/legal/h_to_k/indecent_photographs_of_children/. Accessed 1 May 2016.

Daily Mail. (2009). Cartoon violence "makes children more aggressive." http://www.dailymail.co.uk/news/article-1159766/Cartoon-violence-makes-children-aggressive.html. Accessed 1 May 2016.

Daily Mail. (2012a). *Sex texts epidemic: Experts warn sharing explicit photos is corrupting children.* http://www.dailymail.co.uk/news/article-2246154/Sex-texts-epidemic-Experts-warn-sharing-explicit-photos-corrupting-children.html. Accessed 1 May 2016.

Daily Mail. (2012b). Children grow up addicted to online porn sites: Third of 10-year-olds have seen explicit images. http://www.dailymail.co.uk/news/article-2131799/Children-grow-addicted-online-porn-sites-Third-10-year-olds-seen-explicit-images.html. Accessed 1 May 2016.

Daily Mail. (2014). Student jailed for slapping a sleeping woman in the face with his penis while a friend filmed it on his phone. http://www.dailymail.co.uk/news/article-2803524/Student-jailed-slapping-sleeping-woman-face-penis-friend-filmed-phone.html. Accessed 1 May 2016.

Department for Education. (2015a). *Draft: Keeping children safe in education. Guidance for schools and colleges.* https://www.gov.uk/government/uploads/system/uploads/attachment_data/file/487799/Keeping_children_safe_in_education_draft_statutory_guidance.pdf. Accessed April 2016.

Department for Education. (2015b). *Keeping children safe in education: Proposed changes.* London: Department for Education.

Desai, R. A., Krishnan-Sarin, S., Cavallo, D. & Potenza, M. N. (2010). Video-gaming among high school students: Health correlates, gender differences and problematic gaming. *Pediatrics, 26*(6), 1414–1424.

Education Select Committee. (2014). *Call for evidence: PSHE and SRE in schools.* http://www.parliament.uk/business/committees/committees-a-z/com mons-select/education-committee/news/pshe-and-sre-tor/. Accessed 1 May 2016.

Education Select Committee. (2015). *Education—Fifth Report Life lessons: PSHE and SRE in schools.* http://www.publications.parliament.uk/pa/cm201415/ cmselect/cmeduc/145/145.pdf. Accessed 1 May 2016.

Elliott, J. (1996). School effectiveness research and its critics: Alternative visions of schooling. *Cambridge Journal of Education, 26*(2), 199–223.

Elson, M., & Ferguson, C.J. (2013). Twenty-five years of research on violence in digital games and aggression: Empirical evidence, perspectives, and a debate gone astray. *European Psychologist, 19*, 33–46.

European Union. (2000). Directive 2000/31/EC of the European Parliament and of the Council of 8 June 2000 on certain legal aspects of information society services, in particular electronic commerce, in the Internal Market ("Directive on electronic commerce"). http://eur-lex.europa.eu/legal-con tent/EN/ALL/?uri=CELEX:32000L0031. Accessed 1 May 2016.

Federal Trade Commission. (1998). Children's online privacy protection rule. https://www.ftc.gov/enforcement/rules/rulemaking-regulatory-reform-pro ceedings/childrens-online-privacy-protection-rule. Accessed 1 May 2016.

Ferguson, C.J. (2015). Does media violence predict societal violence? It depends on what you look at and when. *Journal of Communication, 65*, E1–E22.

Griffiths, M. (2000). Does internet and computer 'addiction' exist? Some case study evidence. *Cyberpsychology & Behavior, 3*(2), 211–218.

Horvath, M., Alys, L., Massey, K., Pina, A., Scally, M., & Adler, J. (2013) Basically.. porn is everywhere: A rapid evidence assessment on the effects that access and exposure to pornography has on children and young people. Project Report. Office of the Children's Commissioner for England, London, UK.

International Business Times. (2013). 'Doom' turns 20: We take a look at the game's history. http://www.ibtimes.com/doom-turns-20-we-take-look games-history-1505336. Accessed 1 October 2016.

Internet Watch Foundation. (2015). Emerging patterns and trends report #1 youth-produced sexual content. https://www.iwf.org.uk/assets/media/ resources/Emerging%20Patterns%20and%20Trends%20Report%201%20-% 20Youth-Produced%20Sexual%20Content.pdf. Accessed 1 May 2016.

Kirsh, S. (2006). Cartoon violence and aggression in youth. *Aggression and Violent Behavior, 11*(6), 547–676.

Kocurek, C. (2012). The agony and the exidy: A history of video game violence and the legacy of death race. *Game Studies, 12*(1).

Kyriakides, L., & Campbell, R.J. (2004). School self-evaluation and school improvement: A critique of values and procedures. *Studies in Educational Evaluation, 30*(1), 23–36.

Lacohee, H, Crane, S., & Phippen, A. (2006). *Trust guide: Final report.* http://www.sciencewise-erc.org.uk/cms/assets/Uploads/Project-files/TrustGuide-final-Report.pdf. Accessed May 2016.

Livingstone, S., Haddon, L., Görzig, A., and Ólafsson, K. (2011). *Risks and safety on the internet: The perspective of European children. Full findings.* LSE, London: EU Kids Online.

MacBeath, J. (1999). *Schools must speak for themselves: The case for school self-evaluation.* London: Routledge.

Morgan, N. (2016) *Response to education select committee inquiry in PSHE.* https://www.gov.uk/government/uploads/system/uploads/attachment_data/file/499338/Nicky_Morgan_to_Education_Select_Committee_-_10_Feb_2016–.pdf. Accessed 1 May 2016.

Mortimore, P., & Sammons, P. (1997). *Endpiece: A welcome and a riposte to critics.* In J. White and M. Barber (Eds.), (1997) *Perspectives on school effectiveness and school improvement.* London: Institute of Education, Bedford Way Articles.

Mortimore, P., & Whitty, G. (1997). *Can school improvement overcome the effects of disadvantage?.* London: Institute of Education, Occasional Article.

NoBullying. (2015a). *Jessie Logan—The rest of the story.* http://nobullying.com/jessica-logan/. Accessed 21 April 2016.

NoBullying. (2015b). *The unforgettable Amanda Todd story.* http://nobullying.com/amanda-todd-story/. Accessed 21 April 2016.

Nusche, D., Laveault, D., MacBeath, J., & Santiago, P. (2012). *OECD reviews of evaluation and assessment in education: New Zealand 2011.* OECD Publishing.

"safety. n". OED Online. (2016). Oxford University Press. http://www.oed.com/. Accessed October 2016.

OFCOM. (2011). Children and parents: Media use and attitudes report 2011. http://stakeholders.ofcom.org.uk/binaries/research/media-literacy/oct2011/Children_and_parents.pdf. Accessed 1 May 2016.

OFCOM. (2014). Children and parents: Media use and attitudes report 2014. http://stakeholders.ofcom.org.uk/binaries/research/media-literacy/media-use-attitudes-14/Childrens_2014_Report.pdf. Accessed 1 May 2016.

OFSTED. (2012). Inspecting safeguarding in maintained schools and academies. https://www.gov.uk/government/uploads/system/uploads/attachment_data/file/457203/Inspecting_safeguarding_in_maintained_schools_and_academies_-_a_briefing_for_section_5_inspections.pdf.

Open Rights Group. (2016). *Are you being blocked?* https://www.blocked.org.uk. Accessed 1 May 2016.

Page, A., Cooper, A., Griew, P., & Jago, R. (2010). Children's screen viewing is related to psychological difficulties irrespective of physical activity. *Pediatrics, 126*(5), e1011–e1017.

Perry, C. (2012). *An independent parliamentary inquiry into online child protection.* London: HMSO.

Peterborough Telegraph. (2016). Judge's warning over dangers of "sexting" following Whittlesey case. http://www.peterboroughtoday.co.uk/news/crime/judge-s-warning-over-dangers-of-sexting-following-whittlesey-case-1-7229984. Accessed 1 May 2016.

Phippen, A. (2009). *Sharing personal images and videos among young people.* South West Grid for Learning & University of Plymouth, UK. http://www.swgfl.org.uk/StayingSafe/SextingSurvey. Accessed 1 May 2016.

Phippen, A. (2010). *Online safety policy and practice in the UK—An analysis of 360 degree safe self-review data.* http://swgfl.org.uk/products-services/esafety/resources/online-safety-research/Content/360analysisSept2010(2).pdf. Accessed 21 April 2016.

Phippen, A. (2012a). *Online safety policy and practice in the UK and internationally—An analysis of 360 degree safe/generation safe self-review data 2011.* http://swgfl.org.uk/news/Files/Documents/Online-Safety-Services/Online-Safety-Policy-and-Practice-in-the-UK-and-in.* Accessed 1 May 2016.

Phippen, A. (2012b) *Sexting: An exploration of practices, attitudes and influences.* https://www.nspcc.org.uk/Inform/resourcesforprofessionals/sexualabuse/sexting-pdf_wdf93254.pdf. Accessed 1 May 2016.

Phippen, A. (2013) *UK schools online safety policy and practice assessment 2013: Annual analysis of 360 degree safe self-review data.* http://swgfl.org.uk/products-services/esafety/resources/online-safety-research/Content/Online-Safety-Policy-and-Practice-2013. Accessed 1 May 2016.

Phippen, A. (2014). *UK schools online safety policy and practice assessment 2014 annual analysis of 360 degree safe self-review data.* Exeter: South West Grid for Learning.

Phippen, A., & Ashby, S. (2014). Digital behaviors and people risk: Challenges for risk management. In M. R. Olivas-LujÁN and T. Bondarouk (Eds.), *Social media in strategic management (Advanced series in management, Volume 11)* (pp. 1–26). London: Emerald Group Publishing Limited.

Phippen, A. (2015). *UK schools online safety policy and practice assessment 2015 annual analysis of 360 degree safe self-review data.* Exeter: South West Grid for Learning.

Plymouth Herald (2015). Teenage boy sold sex pictures of his ex, aged 15, to mate for £10. http://www.plymouthherald.co.uk/teenage-boy-sold-sex-pictures-ex-aged-15-mate-10/story-25959544-detail/story.html. Accessed 1 October 2016.

Pring, R. (1996). *Educating persons: Putting education back into educational research. Scottish Educational Review, 27*(2), 101–112.

Rehbein, F., Kleimann, M., & Mößle, T. (2010). Prevalence and risk factors of video game dependency in adolescence: Results of a German nationwide survey. *CyberPsychology, Behaviour and Social Networking, 13*(3), 269–277.

Ringrose, J., Gill, R., Livingstone, S., & Harvey, L. (2012). *A qualitative study of children, young people and 'sexting'—A report prepared for the NSPCC.* National Society for the Prevention of Cruelty to Children.

Ringrose, J., Harvey, L., Gill, R., & Livingstone, S. (2013). Teen girls, sexual double standards and "sexting". Gendered value in digital exchange. *Feminist Theory, 14,* 305–323.

Roberts, Y. (2005). *The one and only.* Australian *Sunday Telegraph Magazine.*

Rosen, J. (2012). The right to be forgotten. *Stanford Law Review Online, 64,* 88.

Schildkampa, K., Visschera, A., & Luytena, H. (2009). The effects of the use of a school self-evaluation instrument. *School Effectiveness and School Improvement, 20*(1), 69–88.

Shewbridge, C., Hulshof, M., & Nusche, D. (2014). *OECD reviews of evaluation and assessment in education: Northern Ireland, United Kingdom.* OECD.

Srinivas, A., White, M., & Omar, H. (2011). Teens texting and consequences: A brief review. *International Journal of Child and Adolescent Health, 4,* 327–331.

Stoll, L. (1992). School self-evaluation: Another boring exercise or an opportunity for growth?. In S. Riddell and S. Brown (Eds.), *School effectiveness research: Its message for school improvement.* Edinburgh: Scottish Education Department/HMSO.

Stone, N. (2011). The "sexting" quagmire: Criminal justice responses to adolescents' electronic transmission of indecent images in the UK and the USA. *Youth Justice, 11*(3), 266–281.

Tang, X. (2013). 2012 the perverse logic of teen sexting prosecutions (and how to stop it). *Boston University Journal of Science and Technology Law, 19*(1), 106.

UK Government. (1978). *The protection of children act 1978.* http://www.legislation.gov.uk/ukpga/1978/37. Accessed 1 May 2016.

UK Government. (2009). The Byron review action plan. http://webarchive.nationalarchives.gov.uk/20130401151715/http://www.education.gov.uk/publications/eOrderingDownload/Byron_Review_Action_Plan.pdf. Accessed 1 May 2016.

UK Government. (2010). *The academies act 2010.* http://www.legislation.gov.uk/ukpga/2010/32/pdfs/ukpga_20100032_en.pdf. Accessed 21 April 2016.

UK Government. (2015a). Criminal justice and courts act 2015. http://www.legislation.gov.uk/ukpga/2015/2/contents/enacted. Accessed 1 May 2016.

UK Parliament. (2016). Parliamentary business: Online safety bill [HL] 2015–2016. http://services.parliament.uk/bills/2015-16/onlinesafety.html. Accessed 21 April 2016.

UN General Assembly. (1989). *Convention on the rights of the child.* United Nations, Treaty Series, vol. 1577, 3., http://www.unicef.org/crc/. Accessed 1 May 2016.

UN General Assembly. (2014). Promotion and protection of the right to freedom of opinion and expression. https://documents-dds-ny.un.org/doc/UNDOC/GEN/N14/512/72/PDF/N1451272.pdf?OpenElement. Accessed 1 May 2016.

Unicef. (2016). *FACTSHEET: A summary of the rights under the convention on the rights of the child*. http://www.unicef.org/crc/files/Rights_overview.pdf

United Nations. (1990, September 2). *Convention on the rights of the child*. In United Nations Treaty Series, vol. 1577, p. 3. New York. http://treaties.un.org/doc/Publication/UNTS/Volume%201577/v1577.pdf. Accessed 21 April 2016.

Ward, V. (2015). Teenage boy added to police database for "sexting." http://www.telegraph.co.uk/news/uknews/crime/11840985/Teenage-boy-added-to-police-database-for-sexting.html. Accessed 21 April 2016.

Whittle, H., Hamilton-Giachritsis, C., Beech, A., & Collings, G. (2013). A review of online grooming: Characteristics and concerns. *Aggression and Violent Behavior, 18*(1), 62–70.

Wired (2009, July 29). Videogame makers propose ratings board to congress. http://www.wired.com/2009/07/dayintech_0729. Accessed 1 May 2016.

Wise, Deborah. (1982). Video-pornography games cause protest. *InfoWorld, 1*, 7. https://books.google.co.uk/books?id=EjAEAAAAMBAJ&lpg=PP1&pg=PA1&redir_esc=y#v=onepage&q&f=false. Accessed 1 May 2016.

Woods, P. (1979). *The divided school*. London, Boston, and Henley: Routledge & Kegan.

Index

© The Author(s) 2017   151
A. Phippen, *Children's Online Behaviour and Safety*,
DOI 10.1057/978-1-137-57095-6